Listening
Myths

Listening
Myths

Applying
Second Language
Research to
Classroom Teaching

Steven Brown

Ann Arbor
University of Michigan Press

ISBN-13: 978-0-472-03459-8

2014   2013   2012   2011   4   3   2   1

Acknowledgments

Very special thanks to:

- Marc Helgesen for nearly thirty years of excellent conversation about listening, ELT, and life. The influence of our work together on several editions of *English Firsthand*, *Practical English Language Teaching: Listening*, and the first edition of *Active Listening* permeates this book. Marc also read a draft of the manuscript.
- Michael Rost for teaching me a great deal of what I know about listening, through his research and also through talking over what must be hundreds of listening tasks in twenty-five years as an editor and writer.

Neither is responsible for my conclusions here.

The English department at Youngstown State University, Ohio, USA, is the antithesis of all those English departments depicted in academic novels; it is sane, supportive and focused on students. Thanks to chair Gary Salvner for his support of my scholarship over the years.

Many of the ideas in this book were tried out at presentations at the JALT conference in 2006 and at several venues in Taiwan in spring 2007 during my time as a visiting professor at Lunghwa University of Science and Technology. Feedback from the participants was helpful.

Thanks also go to Dorolyn Smith, who provided a story for Myth 8 and worked with me on *Active Listening* and to Lionel Menasche for helping me think through the authenticity model presented in Myth 7.

At Youngstown State University, thanks to Rebekah Hoy for bibliographic and editing assistance, for suggestions on a draft of the manuscript, and for keeping another project running smoothly during summer 2010, and to the Youngstown State University School of

Graduate Studies and Research for funding her assistantship. Ellen Wakeford-Banks in Interlibrary Loan at Maag Library helped me a great deal.

Finally, thanks to Kelly Sippell and the terrific staff at the University of Michigan Press. They are always a pleasure to work with.

Contents

Introduction

Reading through the listening research, I was struck time and again by the complaints that listening was under-researched. Of course, researchers often say that sort of thing to boost the importance of their own contribution. However, the fact that listening is under-researched is partially true in the sense that listening research, and practice, has tended to get stuck in grooves, in which hot topics like schema and strategies get extensively discussed and even get transmitted into the classroom as dogma, while topics like bottom-up listening and the role of vocabulary, because they are perceived as unimportant, get ignored. So, the time for a book that questions listening myths has come.

One of the possible reasons that listening has been under-researched is that it fits uneasily into the mainstream second language research paradigm. Listening was for a time seen as the driver of second language acquisition, when comprehension approaches like Krashen's (1982) held sway. And yet even then the focus was on acquisition, not the process of listening itself. Every theory of language acquisition has a place for input, whether listened to or read. However, the actual psycholinguistic process of listening and its development tends to be assumed, except by those who study it professionally. Researchers and classroom teachers tend to assume that listening will develop as proficiency increases. Even programs that have classes dedicated to listening often see listening as lecture listening and the class as a place to teach note-taking. The role of listening in interactive speaking activities like pair work might be addressed, if at all, by teaching clarification language like, *Could you repeat that, please?*

My view is that listening is a skill to be developed, just like any other skill. I think those who say it's enough to teach strategies see only part of the puzzle. Strategies are a piece of the puzzle, but it's a big-kid's puzzle. While many tend to treat listening as something that will emerge from practice activities, others seem to regard listening practice as time-killing. Skills take practice! If the claim for the ineffectiveness of practice is that teachers turn on the audio, ask some questions, and call it teaching listening, well, yes, that's not very effective. It's also not what I would call practice. Perhaps I'm being naïve, and the good practices of years of good colleagues have blinded me to what is really going on. In any event, I hope this book points the way to a principled approach to teaching listening informed by both research and experience.

The Contents lists the eight myths of listening around which this book is based. While I started with the myths, I've tried to write this book as a response to current research and I've let that research drive the internal organization of the chapters. I think the result is a fairly comprehensive look at listening, though because this is a book for a wide audience and because research goes in cycles, there are doubtless areas that are not covered as fully as some would like. A sort of alternative contents that points out some of the themes is given here.

- Listening is a meaning-making activity. (*Myth 1*)
- Listening is an active process that makes use of background knowledge (previous experience, knowledge of topic, situation, and context), as well as knowledge of language forms (vocabulary, grammar, pronunciation, etc.). (*Myth 2*)
- Listening also makes use of bottom-up processes, including phonological and word recognition processes. (*Myth 3*)
- Listening is difficult for many interesting reasons. (*Myth 4*)
- Listening takes many forms. (*Myth 5*)
- Listening is social as well as individual. (*Myth 6*)
- Listening can be taught in many ways in the classroom. (*Myths 7 and 8*)

This book follows the format of other *Myths* books published by the University of Michigan Press. Each chapter begins with **In the Real World,** an anecdote to ground the chapter in teaching and learning. The second part of the chapter looks at **What the Research Says.**

Finally, **What We Can Do** suggests practical activities that logically follow from the research.

The purpose of this book, like its sister volumes in the *Myths* series, is to have a conversation with the reader about applications of research to language teaching. The tone is consciously conversational and informal, meant to replicate that of a teacher's room. So, perhaps an introduction is in order to contextualize the real world anecdotes in each chapter. Feel free to move on to Myth 1 if you're not interested in my background and prejudices.

Cherryland, the unincorporated area of Alameda County, California, where I grew up, was part of the second-largest Portuguese-American enclave in the United States (the largest being in Massachusetts). My mother's family was Portuguese-American, and my great-grandmother spoke with the accent of one who had learned English as an adult. She was a proud American, though, and admonished those who spoke Portuguese on buses, "You in America now. Speak the English!" My family followed the classic American pattern of losing the language in three generations, so my sister and I speak no Portuguese. My father's family was here in colonial times and worked its way across the South until my father moved to California as a teenager. His grandfather spoke French, though whether as an immigrant or a Cajun is unclear.

I got into TESOL by student-teaching an American Studies class at City College of San Francisco that was popular with immigrants as a bridge class between ESL and the required English classes. Soon after, I got a job in a conversation program at the University of California–Berkeley Extension; most of the students were Japanese. Why not come to Japan to teach, they said. Why not, I thought—for a year or two. I went to Japan and stayed ten years. Before leaving, I tried listening to records (records!) and teaching myself Japanese. I succeeded to some extent with a few words and useful phrases. People always ask if I knew Japanese before I moved there. But not knowing Japanese never struck me as an impediment. I thought I'd pick it up. And somehow I did. I left Japan reasonably good at spoken Japanese. I could tell taxi drivers shortcuts to my apartment (this is something Japanese cabbies actually like to talk about) and talk to my dry cleaner about sumo, but my literacy was closest to that of a Japanese fourth grader.

For the first five years in Japan, I taught mostly speaking, as did most foreign teachers at that time. I taught some listening, but the schools mostly saw the teachers' role as giving the students as much speaking practice as possible. For the second five years, while at the University of Pittsburgh English Language Japan Program in Tokyo, I taught the full range of skills: grammar, reading, writing, speaking, pronunciation, and listening. When the program closed and I moved to Pittsburgh to work on my Ph.D., I taught a similarly broad range of classes, though for my time there, I was the supervisor for speaking classes. Now, I teach mostly graduate classes in TESOL, but every semester I also teach a small EAP composition class.

While in Japan, I became interested in materials development. Marc Helgesen invited me onto a textbook project, *English Firsthand*, and we've been working on the project, with editor Michael Rost, as the various editions have continued, for more than 25 years. We've been joined along the way by Thomas Mandeville, Robin Jordan, Ruth Venning, and (currently) John Wiltshier. Marc, Dorolyn Smith, and I also wrote the first edition of *Active Listening*, and Dorolyn and I recently completed a second edition. Marc and I have also written *Practical English Teaching: Listening* in a series of introductions to language teaching edited by David Nunan (Helgesen & Brown, 2007). All of this is to say that I come at listening both as a teacher and as a textbook writer who has written, revised, and thrown out more listening tasks and scripts than I care to count. Yet the whole process continues to fascinate me. I've changed my mind a lot over the years, and some of what I've written in this book probably contradicts what I've produced, and more than likely is at odds with what some of my colleagues believe.

I've studied several languages over the years and will fully agree with anyone who says that listening is hard. I believe that language teachers should constantly strive to understand their students' experiences by learning themselves. I studied Spanish in junior high and high school, Japanese in Japan, and Mandarin Chinese while on a faculty exchange for five months in Taiwan. In between, I took a class in Korean in graduate school and studied a comprehension-based program for learning French. As I write this, I'm back to working on French.

1

Listening is the same as reading.

In the Real World . . .

I took my first foreign language class, Spanish, in seventh grade. It was the 1960s in California and, though I certainly didn't know it then, audiolingualism was the methodology of choice. I remember memorizing dialogues; for years, I could remember isolated snatches of them. I remember reading about culture and seeing Mexican textiles on the walls. What I don't remember is any listening exercises beyond repeating sentences played on reel-to-reel tape.

After exhausting all the Spanish classes at Sunset High, I went on to the University of California at Santa Cruz. My high school Spanish satisfied whatever language requirement was in place at the time, and Spanish classes were at 8 AM on top of a hill, so sloth won out over what really was a fondness for studying languages. Incidentally, despite its current bad reputation, audiolingualism was strong enough to last for years; I can get by in Spanish-speaking countries to this day, as long as I'm asking for the restroom and not trying to discuss philosophy.

At the beginning of the 1980s, I found myself teaching English in Japan. This was the era of the Communicative Revolution—or so we thought. One of the things in the air at the time was the absolute necessity of teaching listening skills. Real skills, real teaching—meaning an exclusive focus in the lesson on how to listen. This may seem obvious now, but it was anything but then. The local TESOL affiliate JALT, the Japan Association for Language Teaching, sponsored numerous presentations on how to teach listening. A major factor generating interest in listening was the fact that so many of our Japanese students were so bad at it. The Japanese educational system was then very focused on teaching students to read English, by which was meant, translate English into Japanese. In order to read English, students were also taught to analyze English grammar. Little oral work was done and virtually no listening tasks; indeed, many classes were predominately in Japanese. As a result, students left high school or university without much knowledge of spoken English and thus had a difficult time understanding what was said to them in English.

So, let's teach them to listen, we thought. The research base, or even the teacher lore, that would tell us how to do this was still slim, but beginning to grow. The University of Michigan Press had published the first American textbook devoted to listening comprehension in 1972 (Morley, 1972). Jack Richards had written what came to be a seminal article on listening in *TESOL Quarterly* (Richards, 1983). By 1985, a survey in the *TESOL Newsletter* reported 76 different listening textbooks being used in North American English language intensive programs (Works, 1985), but that number includes test-preparation materials, course books with some listening, and songbooks, and it reflects a rapid growth of titles in the early 1980s. One of the first listening-oriented JALT presentations I attended was by Dale Griffee, who was working on incorporating listening with English through drama (Griffee, 1982).

There were still plenty of materials that basically had the teacher read a passage and then ask comprehension questions, but some practitioners began to adopt a format of pre-listening, listening, and post-listening.

In either case, basically what we were doing was replicating reading lessons.

What the Research Says . . .

Some Preliminary Definitions ─────

We have long been teaching listening just as we teach reading. That makes a certain amount of sense, since both are more like each other than they are similar to speaking and writing, the other classic language skills. Both reading and listening used to be thought of as passive skills, while speaking and writing were active. That view was abandoned in the 1980s as people began to see, through research, just how active the processes of reading and listening are. At that time, the terms active/passive got replaced with the notions of productive/receptive. I'm not sure that "receptive" does justice to how we listen to other people, though. It may be true that learners are only receiving meaning when they listen to pre-recorded audio, but does "receptive" really characterize the joint meaning-making that goes on during a conversation? Listening to the radio or a lecture is non-reciprocal listening. Participating in conversations and discussion requires reciprocal listening. We can also call reciprocal listening "interactive" or "interactional" listening. Richards (1983) contrasted interactional listening, by which people maintain social contact, with transactional listening, by which people accomplish goals such as buying a train ticket, with relatively little personal connection between speakers.

DIFFERENCES BETWEEN LISTENING AND READING

As I've said, we have taught listening as if it were reading. But are listening and reading the same? At some level, the answer to this question is *no*. There are several differences between listening and reading. For instance, students can skim a text quickly to get a good idea what it's about, but listeners can't skim. The language comes rushing at them. Listening must be done in real time; there is no second chance, unless, of course, the listener specifically asks for repetition. When students read, cognates (words that are similar in two languages) help understanding, but while cognates may look alike on the page, their sounds may be quite different and they may be less useful while listening.

Listening also involves understanding all sorts of reductions of sounds and blending of words (*Whaddayuwannaeat?*). There are false starts (*I, I, uh . . .*) and hesitations (*Um, like . . .*) to be dealt with. Listeners give back-channel cues (*Uh-huh, Really?*) to show they are listening and understanding. Spoken language in general is "looser" than written language; we use a lot of pronouns (*it, that*), string together clauses with conjunctions (*and, but, so*) rather than use subordinate clauses (*while, because*), and rely partly on gestures and body language to get our points across. Rather than define listening negatively against reading, however, let's define it in its own terms, as given in Tables 1 and 2.

TABLE 1: Differences between Listening and Reading

- speed of input
- use of cognates
- reductions and blending of sounds
- false starts and hesitations
- presence of back-channel cues

TABLE 2: Speech vs. Writing Related to Listening

- Speech units tend to be shorter than written units.
- Speech uses more pronouns and generally vaguer language.
- Speech makes use of conjunctions (*and, but, so*) while writing uses subordination, in which dependent clauses are linked to independent clauses with words like *that, which, when,* or *while.*
- Speech is less fluent and filled with redundancies, fillers, and self-corrections.
- Speech uses less standard grammar than writing and more colloquial language, including slang.
- Speech uses gestures and body language to transmit meaning.

A FEW MORE DEFINITIONS

Listening, most basically, is making sense of what you hear. *Hear* is a term with some problems inherent in it, however. Think of the difference between the everyday meanings of *listen* and *hear*. A few years ago, one of my local radio stations ran a series of testimonials from its listeners; one listener said, "I hear you guys everywhere, even when I don't listen." If you listen to something, it implies some degree of focus on your part. In this case, the listener was hearing the radio station in stores and from the windows of others. Her radio was not on; in her mind, she was not listening. You may listen to the radio, but you hear a noise outside. You may hear the birds outside your window, listen for a few seconds, and then stop listening as something else catches your attention.

So perhaps it's better to say that listening is making sense of aural input. What does *make sense* mean? It means that, again, listening is something that takes effort. We use our knowledge of individual pieces of language like sounds, words, and grammatical patterns in concert with our knowledge of the topic, situation, and context to arrive at an understanding of what is being transmitted to us. Because all we know is not necessarily relevant to a given piece of speech, this knowledge implies the selection and sorting of information. Finally, then, listening is a very active process. (See O'Malley, Chamot & Küpper, 1989, pp. 419–422, for a classic definition of listening.)

And yet, if, in the paragraph above, I replaced *listening* with *reading*, *aural* with *written*, and *speech* with *text*, I'd have a pretty decent definition of reading. So maybe the question of the difference between listening and reading lies elsewhere.

But before we go further, perhaps I'd better state the obvious. This entire discussion is in the realm of additional, L2, language learning. If you are reading this from the perspective of a teacher of L1 English speakers, you will see the relationship between oral language and written language differently. You may accept the consensus that Sticht and James (2002/1984, p. 294) enumerate in this way:

(1) oral language skills develop to a fairly high level prior to the development of written language, (2) oral and written language share essentially the same lexicon (vocabulary) and syntax (grammar), and (3) beginning readers draw upon their knowledge of oral language in learning to read.

Sticht and James are clearly talking about young children learning to read in their native language. In an L2 context, particularly in an EFL environment, learning to read English may come before learning to speak it. Many English for Academic Purposes (EAP) students, those attending American universities for example, may be able to handle sophisticated specialized vocabulary and syntax in their academic field, but struggle to understand teenaged servers. Thus, the role of oral abilities and written abilities in language learning, and the connection between them, is not so straightforward in L2 research.

Listening, Reading, and Language Proficiency ———

Since Alderson raised the issue (1984), researchers have been interested in the role our L1 abilities play in our second language. Alderson located the issue in terms of reading research. Do good readers in L1 have a leg up in L2 reading, or must some threshold of general proficiency in the language be crossed before that native language ability can be taken advantage of? Vandergrift (2006) examined the roles of language proficiency and first language listening ability in a group of English-speaking eighth graders studying French. Vandergrift reviewed past studies of reading and came down on the side of those who believe that L1 reading abilities (e.g., efficient skimming, scanning, guessing from context) can't be transferred to L2 when proficiency is low; once learners progress and understand more of the L2, then they are able to make use of L1 abilities (p. 8). In his own study of listening, Vandergrift (2006) concluded that L2 listening comprehension ability is a combination of L1 listening ability and L2 proficiency, but that L2 proficiency contributes more. Furthermore, there were different kinds of questions in the tests that the students were given, and Vandergrift

sees L2 proficiency, particularly vocabulary knowledge, as being important for answering "literal" (specific information) questions (p. 13).
Vandergrift reminds us that just knowing a word is not enough, that
students must also be able to recognize that word when it is spoken, to
match their knowledge with the input. To that end, it helps to have
some idea of what is possible in that particular slot, and teaching
strategies such as using context is therefore necessary. I will have more
to say about strategies in Myth 8.

Comparing Listening and Reading in Research ——

An early study that compared reading and listening was done by Lund
(1991). Lund tested beginning and intermediate university students of
German as a foreign language in the United States using a written text
(a text is a piece of discourse, written or spoken) with oral features and
an interview. One group of students read the text while the other group
heard the same text, as if it were a radio feature story. Each student then
wrote as many of the main ideas and details as possible in five minutes, then heard or read the text, and recalled it again. The ideas in the
text were scored according to a scale of their importance to the text
(main ideas were rated higher than small details). Readers overall
recalled more ideas than listeners did, but there was a difference in the
kinds of ideas recalled. Listeners recalled a higher proportion of the
higher-order, main ideas, than the readers did, while the readers
recalled more details. Also, it seemed that listeners, while understanding a lot of the main ideas, had to fill in the gaps in their understanding by guessing at context, and this led to more erroneous answers.
Lund pointed out that the gaps were often at the word level. Cognates
are not as available for use in listening as they are in reading, because
though they look alike on paper, they sound different when pronounced. Furthermore, when listeners encounter a word they don't
know, they frequently respond by focusing on that word and thus stop
listening to the rest of the text. Lund saw the recall task, in which learners stop between listenings/ readings to write down what they remember, as being potentially a useful classroom activity, at least for

intermediate students, because it allows them to develop an overall meaning for the text and provides an opportunity to work out what they don't know, thereby preparing them for the next listening. Lund also suggests combining reading and listening by using transcripts of the spoken text (sparingly) to increase comprehension. Some teachers also show movies or television shows with subtitles at lunchtime. We will talk more about listening-while-reading later (see pages 11–16).

Park (2004) also compared two groups reading and listening to the same text, in this case through a study of Korean university learners of English. Park reported that listeners performed better on global comprehension questions—those that required inference and synthesizing. Readers did better on factual, local questions. In other words, he confirmed Lund's findings. Park began the study by assessing students' knowledge of the topics and their linguistic knowledge (defined as vocabulary and grammar). Linguistic knowledge was a factor in both groups; those with more knowledge of English, perhaps not surprisingly, performed better on the comprehension questions. Background knowledge had only a moderate effect on reading comprehension, but played a much larger role in listening comprehension, perhaps because the listeners did better on main idea questions and background knowledge helps with those questions. Still, linguistic and background knowledge together only accounted for 14 percent of the variance for the listeners and 20 percent for the readers, which means that something else, we don't know what, explained more than 80 percent of the results.

A comparison of online listening and reading tasks was undertaken by Absalom and Rizzi (2008). Six stories, each less than five minutes long, were recorded from Italian radio. The audio was transcribed to form written texts. Fourteen students volunteered to study one text a week in two groups, listeners and readers. There were a number of interesting results. First, listeners went deeper into the material in the sense that they went beyond the text to look up topics on the internet and look up words in a dictionary. They seemed to want to understand the material more fully than any of the readers did; none of the readers used outside sources, even though they wound up giving incorrect answers. Absalom and Rizzi characterize this as a "deep" approach and contrast it with the surface approach of the readers, who seemed to want to just finish the task. They say that perhaps the readers were comfortable with their understanding and had strategies for reading text, while the listeners were anxious about listening. Even though the listeners either chose or needed to work harder, they also stayed more motivated than the readers did throughout the study and, ultimately, remembered more information than the readers.

In a study in which the same learners both read and listened to the same passage, within a two-week period, advanced university students of Spanish recalled the same amount of information in either modality, while intermediate students recalled significantly more main ideas when they read, but not significantly more details (Mecartty 2001). Readers recalled more information from the beginning and middle of the text, while listeners recalled more information overall (and more main ideas) from the end, perhaps suggesting further research.

In a study that was primarily concerned with acquisition of Spanish verb morphology, Lesser (2004) found that readers recalled more ideas than listeners.

Thus, classroom studies show that listeners and readers have different experiences with the same material. Research used in developing a placement test at the University of California at Los Angeles (Song, 2008) suggests that listening and reading share some processes but differ slightly in others. Song used a structural equation modeling approach, which tried to build a model using hypothesized factors, to investigate whether listening and reading consist of subskills and, if so, the same subskills. This is knowledge that helps test-makers construct tests that really measure what students know.

Basically, it was found that both listening and reading are made of subskills, but the pies are cut differently. Listening can be divided into Topic, Details, and Inference; that is, a person with high scores in those three subskills would be a good listener. Reading divides into what Song calls Explicit and Implicit factors. Explicit factors are Topic and Details, and Implicit is another name for Inference. This is to say that the study could not cleanly separate the roles of Topic and Details among readers. Song (2008) is reluctant to make a definitive statement on the difference between listening and reading but suggests that both can be fundamentally defined as "comprehension plus decoding." Both have comprehension processes in common but different decoding processes. That is, the path to comprehension is different.

"Comprehension plus decoding" is actually a good way to characterize listening. Decoding is the process of breaking up the speech stream into recognizable words, which are then held in working memory and tied to what Anderson and Lynch (1988, p. 13) call "information sources in comprehension." These sources are schematic knowledge (background knowledge and procedural knowledge of how language is used in discourse); context (knowledge of situation and co-text, what has been said before and will be said); and systemic knowledge (knowledge of the language system, semantic, syntactic and phonological). More on all of this in Myths 2 and 3.

Finally, though listening and reading share many comprehension processes, they shouldn't unthinkingly be treated as the same in terms of research and pedagogy, as we have done at certain times. There are differences between listening and reading in the way that input is taken in for processing, partly attributable to the differences in speech and writing. Readers can remember more, and remember more details, because the text is fixed. Readers can go back to it. Listeners have to construct the text as they listen. They have to make use of knowledge from other sources and may come away with more of the gist. Table 3 summarizes the comparisons.

TABLE 3: Listening and Reading Compared

Readers recall more ideas overall.	Lund (1991), Lesser (2004)
Listeners remember more ideas.	Absalom & Rizzi (2008)
Listeners recall more main ideas or do better at main idea questions, while readers recall more details or did better at detail questions.	Lund (1991), Park (2004)
Listeners display deeper learning and more motivation.	Absalom & Rizzi (2008)
Listening and reading share comprehension processes but differ in decoding.	Song (2008)

Listening while Reading ——

What happens when we combine listening and reading? Reading while listening—for example, following along while the teacher reads aloud—is probably something we have all experienced in elementary school. Brown, Waring, and Donkaewbua (2008) tested the efficacy of listening while reading as an L2 vocabulary acquisition tool versus reading only and listening only. Though the Japanese university students liked listening-while-reading best as a method, none of the methods led to significant vocabulary gains.

The Taiwanese university students who participated in Chang's study (2009) also liked the listening-while-reading condition, compared to listening only. They thought it was easier, and they claimed they paid more attention. Gains in comprehension for the listening-while-reading condition over the listening-only condition were very modest, however, as they were in Woodall (2010). Woodall compared a group that read a children's novel (*Charlotte's Web*) to one that listened to a professional recording of the book while reading. Students had control of the audio. There were weekly comprehension quizzes, and the listening-while-reading group outscored the reading-only group in four of the eight quizzes.

Perhaps the best use of reading-while-listening to stories (and all of these studies focused on stories) is to model for students how words chunk together. Non-proficient readers tend to read word-by-word and essentially lose the overall meaning. If they can listen to texts read by fluent readers, they may, over time, shape their own reading into larger chunks. See Table 4.

One study that was actually done to test the role of advance organizers (pre-reading/listening activities) also gave information about listening while reading. Chung (1999) found that there was no statistical difference between a group of Chinese-speaking technical school students who viewed a video with English language captions and a group that viewed with captions and also listened to a summary of the video before viewing. There was a significant difference between both of these groups and a group that received the summary only, with the summary being less effective at aiding comprehension. The captions seemed to make the difference. This in fact supports listening while reading. We will look at the effectiveness of captions more in Myth 5.

TABLE 4: Studies on Listening while Reading

Learners enjoyed the activity.	Chung (1999), Brown et al. (2008), Chang (2009)
There were gains in comprehension.	Chung (1999), Woodall (2010)
There were no significant gains in vocabulary acquisition.	Brown et al. (2008)
There were no significant gains in comprehension.	Chang (2009)

Some other interesting classroom activities that link listening and readings are explored next.

What We Can Do . . .

So, what does this mean for the listening classroom (and when I say that, it's shorthand for "all the classrooms in which listening is taught" and doesn't refer just to listening classes). If comprehension is a process shared by listening and reading, then perhaps one reinforces the other pedagogically. This is the rationale behind the common use of reading aloud in L1 elementary schools. While the research on listening while reading in L2 is mixed, we do know that listeners and readers understand different parts of the input differently, for example, main ideas and details. Thus, I believe we're led to a prescription to combine listening and reading in the classroom through the use of transcripts and dialogues.

1. Exploit the reading-listening connection through use of transcripts.

Using transcripts (written versions of the listening material) is controversial for many teachers. In the past, I would have encouraged you to hide the transcripts, maybe even burn them. I would have said that they encouraged bad listening habits, that students will not learn to listen as long as they can read what is said. I would have pointed out that no one gives us the transcript of a conversation, that we must tough it out and get what we can. As we listen more, we get better at it and develop strategies for coping with what we don't know.

All that is true to some extent. It just doesn't have to be shouted from the rooftops or be seen as dogmatically. What has become increasingly clear to me is that the classroom is not the real world, nor should it be. It is a place for growth.

I have also come to believe in the power of repetition, not in the mindless listen-and-repeat of behaviorism and audiolingualism, but careful, principled practice. As we have noted, one of the characteristics of speech is its fleeting nature. We can deal with the transient nature of the listening experience through playing the audio file over and over, but the unprepared students are really not very likely to get more out of the sixth listening than they are of the second. To be sure, there are some things that can be heard better on a second or third listening, but learners top out pretty quickly. (Though I note that to this day, largely because of better audio, I sometimes suddenly understand words of a song I have never understood despite having listened to it for 40 years.) But there are other ways to repeat the input besides playing the audio again and again, and transcripts are one way.

Transcripts are for me what Vygotksy and his followers call "psychological tools" (Kozulin, 1998). A shovel is a physical tool that helps you dig a hole to plant a tree (to use some jargon, it mediates between you and your task). A string around your figure to remember to take out the garbage is a psychological tool. Potentially, a transcript is a tool that can help learners work on repetitive tasks like multiple listenings—and, I would argue, improve the experience of those tasks.

I would definitely not provide the transcript for every listening task, mostly because it encourages the students to think that they need to understand everything. They don't, as we will see. But if you have students who want to do repeated listening or want to practice speaking, occasionally providing a script is probably a good idea.

WAYS TO USE SCRIPTS

Here are some ways you can use or adapt listening scripts (this assumes, by the way, the publisher provides permission to copy the scripts).

- One obvious use of scripts is for pronunciation work. Learners can mark the stressed words they hear. More advanced learners can predict the stressed words and listen to the audio to check.
- Scripts can be used for do-it-yourself pairwork. One member of the pair (A) can delete words and hand the blacked-out script to a partner (B), who has to listen and write the missing words as A reads the script, or as both listen to the audio.

- Some learners find it useful to try to match the speed and intonation of the audio as they read the script.
- If the focus of your class is on language forms, grammatical or other, learners can highlight the forms in the script. This doesn't have to be a grammar exercise; they can listen to the audio and highlight occurrences of whichever sound you choose or sounds you want them to contrast. They can then put away the script and listen again, raising their hand or tapping their desk when they hear the target form.
- Finally, because so many listening scripts are dialogues, they offer interactive speaking practice.

2. Focus on interactive listening by using dialogues.

Students reading dialogues to each other is another example of the connection between reading and listening. As I will say in greater detail later (see Myth 5), we limit our students' experiences with listening when all we offer them are dialogues. On the other hand, as I will also say in more detail later, much of our social action is dialogic, and students need interactive listening as much or more than they need to listen to recorded audio (see Myth 6).

Dialogues from listening scripts offer us a great deal of extra practice material. It seems a waste not to exploit them. Here are ten options for varying dialogues. Some of them are more focused on listening while others are focused on speaking or even reading. It is up to you to use the versions that best address your class goals.

WAYS TO VARY DIALOGUES IN PAIRS

Note that all these assume students will have heard the audio at least once. They are now practicing.

- Use "read and look up." Learners can only speak when they are looking at their partner. They can look at the dialogue as often as necessary, but when they are speaking, they must be looking up.

- One partner makes mistakes on purpose, which the other partner must catch. This can be done while both partners are reading or from memory as a listening task, as one reads and the other listens (after hearing the original).
- Hand out the dialogue in pieces, with each turn on a different slip of paper. Assign pairs to reconstruct the dialogue. This can be done with each partner having half of the slips. They cannot see each other's slips but instead must listen.
- Partners extend the story. What happens next? They can perform their endings for the class.
- Personalize the dialogue. Learners substitute their names and personal information (likes, etc.) for the textbook's characters.
- Read the original, and then put it aside and perform a role play based on what is remembered.
- One student changes the dialogue, and the other must follow, making adjustments.
- Use voice variations: loud/soft, high/low, etc.
- Vary the physical aspects: sit back to back; stand and step back after each line; stand in lines and change partners to repeat the dialogue.
- In two pairs, A1 whispers the lines to A2, who does the speaking. B1 and B2 do the same.

TABLE 5: Review of Listening-Reading Connections in the Classroom

- Teacher reads the transcript; students follow along.
- One student reads the transcript; others follow along.
- Transcript used for work on sentence stress.
- Blank-filling with transcripts.
- Find the form in the transcript.
- Students read/listen to dialogues in various ways.

2

Listening is passive.

In the Real World . . .

Fast forward ten years. I left Japan and took the Trans-Siberian railroad from Beijing to Moscow and went on to spend some time in Europe. While in Vienna, I went to the national art museum, where I decided to buy some post cards. As travelers do, I added up the purchase in my head to make sure I was giving the clerk a reasonable amount. (You wouldn't believe how angry you can make a Beijing taxi driver by inadvertently requiring a huge amount of change.) I figured the cost was 16 schillings. I put a 20-schilling bill on the counter. The clerk opened the cash register, looked in, and said something to me in German, which I don't speak. Without thinking, I reached in my pocket and gave her "a one." She smiled and gave me a five. My years of buying things had made me aware of the limited possibilities of her response. She had to be saying she was out of change.

Of course, this doesn't always work. You may not know the routine. Coming back late from the airport not so long ago, I stopped at a chain steak restaurant, which I put into the "restaurant" and not "fast food" category. I entered the wrong door and sat without service for quite a while until a server told me I had to pay first and give my receipt to her in order to get something to eat.

You may also think you have the right topic, but don't. I was recently in Pittsburgh to see a friend. It had been several months since we'd talked. As many American academics do, we each have an older house that requires pretty constant upkeep. We often share home improvement conversations. As we were driving to lunch, she asked, "How's your health?" I said, "I'm thinking of doing some work in the front yard." She looked at me, laughed, and said, extra clearly, "Health." In the time I'd last seen her, my health (recovery from an operation) had improved so much that I'd put it out of my mind. On the drive over, I had been planning spring home projects, and my mind was on that, so I answered a question that hadn't been asked.

Sometimes it's what you're ready to hear, not what you really hear.

What the Research Says . . .

One very important idea for teaching listening is that listening courses must make use of students' prior knowledge to improve listening comprehension (Long, 1989). To make this idea clear, I'll introduce several concepts from the cognitive view of language learning.

We have known at least since the 1930s (Bartlett, 1932) that people's prior knowledge has an effect on their cognition. Prior knowledge is organized in *schemata* (the plural form of *schema*): abstract, generalized mental representations of our experience that are available to help us understand new experiences (Anderson, 1994). Another way to look at this phenomenon is the idea of *scripts* (Schank & Abelson, 1977). My Austrian example was part of a "cashier script." There are all sorts of scripts. For example, everyone who has been to a restaurant knows that there is a predictable sequence of questions involved in ordering a meal. In the United States these have to do with whether you want soup or salad, the kind of dressing on the salad, choice of side dishes, etc. Even if you do not hear a question, perhaps because the restaurant is too noisy, you can guess from your place in the script what the server is probably asking. Unfortunately, this script does not transfer perfectly from country to country because the routine is slightly different in each place. However, when traveling in another country and eating in a restaurant, you can make certain assumptions about the kinds of questions that will be asked. If food has been ordered but drinks have not, and the server asks another question, you might fairly predict that the question is about the choice of drinks, based on your prior knowledge of what happens in restaurants. Indeed, successful language learners can often be separated from unsuccessful language learners by their ability to contextualize their guesses and use their prior knowledge in this way.

Many theorists divide schemata into text schemata and content schemata. *Text schemata* refer to knowledge of the way discourse works and to story grammars (All fairy tales are alike in some way, as are all detective stories.) *Content schemata* refer to knowledge of the world or of the topic at hand. Some have claimed that content schemata are more useful for comprehension, while others think that the kind of schemata one relies on has to do with learning style (Long, 1989). Actually, both are needed.

The idea of prior knowledge is one part of the cognitive model of language processing. That model says that when people listen or read, they process the information they hear/read both top-down and bottom-up. Top-down processing means using prior knowledge and experiences; we know certain things about certain topics and situations and use that information to understand. Bottom-up processing means using the information we have about sounds, word meanings, and discourse markers like *first, then,* and *after that* to assemble our understanding of what we read or hear one step at a time. In reality, of course, the process is interactive; both types of processing are used, and it is difficult to separate the two types categorically.

Students obviously need both bottom-up and top-down processing skills in listening. Students must hear some sounds (bottom-up processing), hold them in their working memory long enough (a few seconds) to connect them to each other, and then interpret what they've just heard before something new comes along. At the same time, listeners are using their background knowledge (top-down processing) to determine meaning with respect to prior knowledge and schemata. They also use what has already been said to put the new information in context.

TABLE 6: Review of Some Definitions

> **Top-down processing:** using prior knowledge (schemata, scripts) to organize possible interpretations of the input
>
> **Bottom-up processing:** assembling meaning from individual sounds, words, grammatical patterns, and other bits of language
>
> **Text (or formal) schemata:** knowledge of discourse patterns (comparison/contrast, cause/effect) and story grammars (folk tales, detective stories)
>
> **Content schemata**: knowledge of the world or of topics

At this point, there is a need to introduce one more concept from cognitive psychology: the human as a limited processor of information. Think of the ability to pat your head and rub your stomach at the same time. This is an interesting analogy to apply to listening because it is first a matter of individual differences: some people can do this better than others. So with listening. Some people are inherently better listeners than others. But even the best listeners, as anyone who has studied or taught a language knows, can have a difficult time. Beginners, especially, are psychologically trying to rub their stomachs and pat their heads at the same time. At beginning levels of language learning, students are thinking about everything they say; it requires a great deal of effort to speak even the simplest utterance. They are often listening word by word, and if they don't know a word, they stop. As proficiency improves, certain aspects of language become automatic, and speaking and listening become less of an effort (DeKeyser, 2001).

This is what we are doing when we prepare learners for listening activities. We are trying to ease the processing burden that they face. Especially at a beginning level, language learners have very few automatic processes at their disposal. They process sounds and recognize words with great effort. This effort strains their working memory resources. Working memory is the place that allows input to be held for processing. One way that extra resources are made available is knowledge of the topic. Tyler (2001) tested the effect of providing the topic on working memory. He compared the performance of native English speakers and English language learners while they listened to a text and simultaneously checked calculations (a way to put a burden on working memory). Subjects were instructed to verify that answers to arithmetic calculations were correct while simultaneously trying to remember the story for later recall. Each subject did a calculation task without hearing the story and another while listening. The difference between the two scores was thus a measure of working memory; a greater difference between the scores shows more stress on working memory.

Providing the topic of the story reduced demand on working memory, and did so more for non-native speakers of English than native speakers. Neither group scored significantly different from each other when provided the topic, nor were native speakers greatly affected by absence of the topic. However, if non-native listeners did not know the topic, they performed significantly worse. Working memory consumption was greater. Without the topic, the input alone had to be relied on. The topic had to be found within the input, and the details had to be remembered at the same time. Listening is indeed a very active process, not passive at all.

Research on Schemata in Listening ——

The amount of research on the role of schema activation in listening comprehension, at least compared to schema activation in reading comprehension, is relatively small. Researchers have consistently seen that schema activation can play an important role in reading research, and from that fact we have reasoned that it must play a part in listening comprehension as well. Research in schemata and listening has looked at whether schemata influence comprehension, and, if so, what activities are best at facilitating comprehension. The research has almost accidentally also found that repetition of input is effective in facilitating comprehension.

ARE SCHEMA ACTIVATION ACTIVITIES EFFECTIVE?

Students come to class as members of a society and a culture, and this membership has a role in their listening comprehension. The role of culture, specifically religion, was tested by Markham and Latham (1987). They looked at three groups in a university English language program: Christians, Muslims, and those who were "religion-neutral." The students heard two passages, one on Christian prayer rituals and the other on Muslim prayer rituals. They heard both passages twice and, first, in between the two listenings, then after the second listening, wrote as much as they could remember. Christians recalled more main ideas and made fewer mistakes on the Christian passage than either the Muslims or the religiously neutral. Muslims recalled more main ideas and made fewer mistakes on the Muslim passage than either of the two other groups.

It was life experience rather than culture that was of interest to Long (1990). She looked at 188 intermediate Spanish learners in the Unites States. She was interested in the role of schemata, as well as how linguistic knowledge interacted with prior knowledge. Students heard two listening passage adapted from authentic articles, one on a gold rush in Ecuador (of which they presumably had little knowledge) and the other on the rock band U2 (of which presumably they had some knowledge). Before listening, knowledge of gold rushes, including the 1848 California gold rush, and knowledge of rock bands were assessed. After listening twice, students summarized the passages in English and were also given a checklist of ideas that were mentioned in the text, interwoven with ideas that weren't in the text. They had to select which they had heard. Students recalled more ideas from the U2 passage than from the gold rush passage. For the gold rush passage, some students mixed ideas from the California gold rush with the Ecuadorean one. (Imposing schema on a text can be a problem.) For the gold rush text, there was a moderate correlation between previous grades in Spanish class and performance on the recall. That is, students who had better linguistic knowledge could overcome their lack of schemata. There was no such effect for the U2 passage.

Life experience also was a factor for Schmidt-Rinehart (1994). Spanish students at three levels at an American university recalled more from a spontaneous lecture given by a native Spanish speaker on a familiar topic than an unfamiliar one. The familiar topic, Hispanic universities, was addressed in the textbook, while the custom of strolling in the park was not. There were significant effects for familiarity and level, but no interaction; that is, students at each level understood more than those at the level below, but all students scored higher on the familiar topic.

In a study that was primarily interested in acquisition of Spanish verb morphology (Lesser, 2004), listeners comprehended more information from texts with familiar topics. When they listened to passages with unfamiliar topics, their comprehension was improved by pausing between ideas in the audio.

As we have seen, studies often compare schemata to other factors involved in listening, such as linguistic knowledge and pausing. The roles of speech modification, proficiency, and schemata were assessed by Chiang and Dunkel (1992). Three hundred and eighty-eight Chinese learners of English were divided into high-intermediate and low-intermediate groups. They heard texts in one of four conditions involving familiar/unfamiliar topics and modified/unmodified language. The language was modified by introducing redundancies, repetitions, and elaborations. The topics were either Confucius and Confucianism (familiar) or the life of the Amish (unfamiliar). Prior knowledge or topic familiarity had a positive effect on the comprehension of both groups, but only the high-intermediate students benefitted from the internal repetition and redundancies, perhaps because the low-intermediate students, instead of hearing restatement, heard only more language to be processed. We will re-visit and expand the topic of modifying language in Myth 4.

WHAT KINDS OF ACTIVITIES ARE EFFECTIVE?

So far, we can conclude that schema does have a role in making listening comprehension easier. But what kinds of pre-listening activities are effective?

The role of visual support has been a subject of interest. Mueller (1980) looked at the usefulness of pictures as advance organizers in university German classes. Advance organizers are essentially schema-building activities. Mueller divided his beginning classes into pre-viewers, post-viewers, and non-viewers and found that students who were shown a picture either before hearing a listening passage or after hearing the passage did better on a comprehension test than the control group that did not see the picture. The pre-viewers did better than the post-viewers, however. Mueller hypothesized that the picture allowed the students to activate prior knowledge. By understanding the overall context, students were also able to reject wrong hypotheses about the listening passage and better able to guess unfamiliar words. Their interest was also aroused, so perhaps they paid better attention than they might otherwise have. Perhaps it was also the interest factor that helped the post-viewers; it's hard to explain otherwise. When Mueller repeated the experiment with more proficient students, he found no significant differences between any of the more advanced groups, leading him to believe that visuals are probably most appropriate with beginners or when students cannot otherwise form a context for their listening.

In a study of video comprehension by American beginning students of French, Herron, Hanley, and Cole (1995) discovered that a combination of description (six sentences that previewed the video) and pictures that were related to, but did not illustrate the sentences, was superior to the description alone in facilitating comprehension and retention of the information.

Ginther (2002) made a distinction between "context" and "content" visuals. Context visuals set the stage; they are general depictions, for example, of students talking to a teacher. Content visuals more closely illustrate the actual content of the audio. Content visuals facilitated comprehension in the study, while context visuals actually had a small negative effect, perhaps because they activated the wrong schema.

Wilberschied and Berman (2004) investigated the differential roles of verbal and visual previews in elementary school classes teaching Chinese to American students. Over the course of 14 lessons, they gave two groups of children either written summaries of the videos they were about to watch or written summaries illustrated with still photos captured from the videos. The words-plus-pictures significantly improved comprehension scores for the third graders, but not as much for the fifth graders, recalling Mueller's finding that pictures had a greater effect on beginners.

A similar study was done with EFL learners in Taiwan by Chang and Read (2007). In their case, there were four conditions: visual support in the form of pictures that illustrated the audio; written support in the form of a short L1 text; repetition of the texts; and a control group that received no pre-listening. Students listened to three passages from a textbook, and each of four classes (a total of 140 students) experienced all conditions. The most effective tool to increase comprehension was simply playing the audio twice; repetition increased comprehension 18 percent from the control baseline. The visual and written support had similar results, but they only increased comprehension by 11 percent. Student opinion was also surveyed to see which activities were liked, and students rated the repetition as most effective. They perceived that the visual support was more helpful than the written support, even though it really wasn't.

While visual support might have benefits especially for beginning students, there are other possibilities for pre-listening activities. Berne (1995) compared three groups of university Spanish students in the United States. Two groups used pre-listening activities, and the third was a control group that completed an unrelated activity. The first group used a question preview, in which students studied the comprehension questions and possible multiple choice answers. The second used a vocabulary preview, in which students viewed a list of ten key Spanish words from the story and their English equivalents. They listened to a videotaped lecture without taking notes. They were given a comprehension test and asked to recall as much as they could. Then they listened again and were tested again. There were no significant differences in the scores based on the type of pre-listening activity. There was a small advantage for the question activity, but it was not statistically significant. There were gains after the repetition of the material for all groups.

Berne's study was replicated in a Taiwanese context by Chung (2002) and in an Arabic as a foreign language context by Elkhafaifi (2005a). Chung added a condition in which the question preview was combined with a vocabulary preview. This condition of both (question and vocabulary preview) was markedly more effective for the learners who were considered high achievers, while all three conditions (question preview, vocabulary preview, and both) were effective for low achievers. There was a task effect: the question preview was as effective as *both*, the combined preview, when students answered multiple choice questions, but for open-ended questions, the combined preview had the best results. This suggests that the pre-listening and listening task might need to be considered together.

Elkhafaifi (2005a) found both question preview and vocabulary preview were better than no preview at all, but that the question preview performed better than the vocabulary preview on the first listening. When the audio was repeated, all groups, even the control group, which had had no preview, increased their scores. That is, simple repetition was effective in increasing comprehension.

Repetition is good for comprehension. Chang and Read (2006) investigated a number of ways to facilitate comprehension. They found that topic preparation in Chinese (the study was done in Taiwan) and repetition of the input were most effective in increasing comprehension scores. Repetition worked better for higher-proficiency students, while topic preparation was beneficial for all levels. Students themselves were most concerned about vocabulary that they didn't know, but simply providing students with vocabulary lists as a pre-listening activity was the least effective method of support and actually had a negative effect on higher-proficiency learners. It's possible that this negative effect was a result of the lists activating the wrong schemata, but it's difficult to say.

Iimura (2007) reported that repetition improved performance on both global (main idea) and local (detail) comprehension questions at all levels of proficiency. Sakai (2009) also found that repetition facilitated comprehension and did so for both high- and low-proficiency learners.

The studies are summarized in Table 7. Basically, we know that pre-listening activities are effective in increasing listening comprehension, compared to no activity. We also know that certain activities are more effective than others, at least at a given time in a given place. It seems logical that the pre-task might need to change based on the aural text and/or the listening task itself. There may be times when visuals, a question preview, or vocabulary preview might be most effective, though I don't think you can go wrong with any of them. You might even use them all. How many pre-listening activities you do depends on how much time you have.

It's also clear that repetition of the input is important. Students would like us to repeat until they understand every single word, but I don't think that's practical, possible or, ultimately, likely. Jensen and Vinther (2003) suggest that fatigue sets in as early as the third listening.

Text Structure and Comprehension ——

Carrell's classic study of content and formal (textual) schemata (1987) in reading has generated a number of listening studies. Weissenreider (1987) found that L1 English learners of Spanish used both content and textual schemata while listening to authentic news programs. Their content schemata included their knowledge of the topics of the stories. Their textual schemata was their knowledge of how newscasts are organized generally.

Tudor and Tuffs (1991) looked at one specific type of formal schema, the problem/solution mode of organization, and compared it to content-schemata knowledge of English business. Their subjects were advanced English learners in a Belgian university's business administration program, divided into three groups—formal, content, and no schema. The students listened once and took notes, and then answered comprehension questions after completing a summary from the notes. Both formal and content schemata aided comprehension, compared to the no-schema group, though having formal schemata, knowing what form the text will take, led to slightly higher scores.

TABLE 7: Studies on Schemata and Listening Comprehension

Prior knowledge has a positive effect on comprehension.	Mueller (1980), Markham & Latham (1987), Weissenreider (1987), Long (1990), Tudor & Tuffs (1991), Chiang & Dunkel (1992), Schmidt-Rinehart (1994), Herron et al. (1995), Chung (2002), Ginther (2002), Wilberschied & Berman (2004), Berne (1995), Elkhafaifi (2005a), Chang & Read (2006, 2007), Lesser (2004)
Proficiency effects found beginners and more advanced students may react differently to the kind of pre-listening activity.	Mueller (1980), Long (1990), Chiang & Dunkel (1992), Chung (2002), Wilberschied & Berman (2004), Chang & Read (2006)
Visuals are effective as advance organizers (with caveats).	Mueller (1980), Herron et al. (1995), Ginther (2002), Wilberschied & Berman (2004), Chang & Read (2007)
Question previews are effective.	Berne (1995), Chung (2002), Elkhafaifi (2005)
The combination of question and vocabulary preview is effective.	Chung (2002)
Repetition of input is effective.	Berne (1995), Elkhafaifi (2005a), Chang & Read (2006, 2007), Iimura (2007), Sakai (2009)

Research questions are frequently linked with specific methodologies, as will be shown throughout the book. I will comment on research methods when they are particularly prominent in a line of research (see Table 8).

TABLE 8: Methodology: Researching and Measuring Comprehension

You might have noticed that studies that measure comprehension typically use one of two measures. They may use some sort of test, either multiple choice or open-ended questions. They may instead use some form of recall, writing a summary, for example. Many studies allow the subjects to write the summary in their native language, but this assumes that the researcher either shares a language with the subjects or has access to a translator. This may not always be possible, and subjects may be required to use the target language in their summaries. Studies that require subjects to write extended responses in the target language are often criticized because the subject's proficiency, or lack of it, may have an effect on the report, potentially giving a false account of how much was really comprehended.

We have seen that background knowledge plays a very important part in listening comprehension. Let me link that fact to the myth, in case it's not clear yet. Listening is active, rather than passive, because listeners, by using background knowledge, are constructing meaning, not receiving it.

What We Can Do . . .

The research is clear: activating prior knowledge leads to gains in comprehension. It is less clear exactly what kinds of preview activities are most effective. Many studies found proficiency effects, meaning that beginners and more advanced students made different use of schema activation tasks. There are also intriguing findings about the role of repetition in comprehension. But the best advice I can give you is to always do a pre-listening activity.

1. Always do a pre-listening task.

There are two kinds of pre-listening activities. One requires top-down processing by using what students know about the topic. If the reading is about a famous person, for example, the pre-listening task might require students to list as many things as they can about that person. The second kind of pre-listening task works more on bottom-up listening skills by pre-teaching new vocabulary and other word- and sentence-level knowledge that students might need to know before reading

It's important to remember that we don't want to spend a lot of time doing the pre-task. Let's always keep in mind that the average listening input is at most three or four minutes long. Even though pre-listening is important, we need to keep a sense of proportion and not spend an hour preparing for three minutes.

In the context of a listening class, one could take the following approach. Let's assume the topic is giving directions. The task might be to listen to people asking for and receiving directions in the setting of a downtown. The goal is to give students practice in listening for two vocabulary sets, prepositions of location and buildings. Students are likely to know at least some of these words. Others they probably don't know. A pre-listening task should probably have two parts, then. Students should have an opportunity to learn vocabulary items (and perhaps structures like *Turn left* and *Go straight*) they don't know but that they will need to successfully complete the task. But it is just as important to give the students the opportunity to use what they already know, their prior knowledge, to help them do the task. An ideal situation would be to both activate students' schemata and also specifically pre-teach any vocabulary you felt they wouldn't know—*and* that would be critical for completing the task (remember that they don't need to understand everything). Why not just pre-teach vocabulary and forget the schema activation? After all, it would be quicker. It's an issue of motivation. Giving students a chance to activate their prior knowledge (say in this case by brainstorming words for things that are found downtown) is not just helpful to comprehension. It also motivates students by showing them how much they know and how much control they can have over their learning.

Let me take a moment to back away from the downtown example and make my advice more generic, so that that you can adapt tasks that you find in your textbooks or make listening tasks yourself. For any given listening task, you can assign these three tasks:

1. What's the topic?
2. Write five things you know about the topic.
3. Look at the word list. Check the words you know.

The first two steps attempt to get students thinking about the topic and what they know about it. The third step deals with any word list present on the page or with any pre-teaching of vocabulary the teacher cares to do. If there is no word list, focus on the choices or answers that are on the page, or pull some words from the script and write them on the board.

Most textbooks feature extensive illustrations, which many teachers think of as decoration. In fact, good illustrations support the task and can be used before students listen to help them guess the content of the audio. They can predict words they might hear by looking at the pictures and writing the words next to them:

- Look at the pictures. Write words.

Next, students should look at the choices on the page. How many choices do they have for each item? What is the most important word in each choice?

- Look at the choices you have.

Table 9 lists five things a student can do before listening.

TABLE 9: Five Things to Do before Listening

1. Look at the page. What's the topic?
2. Write five things you know about the topic.
3. Look at the word list. Check the words you know.
4. Look at the pictures. Write words for what you see.
5. Look at the answer choices you have. What's the most important word in each choice?

2. Make sure to include bottom-up as well as top-down pre-listening tasks.

Historically, listening textbooks have focused on schema activation activities. They are reasonably easy to construct, and they are very important. However, recently textbooks are including more bottom-up work, in vocabulary in particular, but also in pronunciation and grammar. I will have much more to say about bottom-up processes and tasks in the next two chapters, but here's a preview.

PRE-TEACHING VOCABULARY

I will have more to say about the role of vocabulary in Myth 4, but I want to introduce the topic here to place it in the context of pre-teaching. According to Nation (2001), students need to know 95 percent of words in the input for "reasonable" comprehension and to have a chance at guessing unknown words from context. Nation says 98 percent would be even better. So while students don't need to know all the words, they need to know a lot.

What's the best way to give students those words? We have depended a lot in recent years on students guessing vocabulary in context, but that is a very difficult thing to do, especially if you are missing a lot of words. Students simply need to be taught more vocabulary. Folse (2004) makes the point that, although word lists as a teaching tool have been criticized in recent years, there is absolutely nothing wrong with them. He cites a study by Laufer and Shmueli (1997) that showed that words presented in lists (or in sentences) were remembered better than words in text. But, Folse cautions against semantic sets, like superordinates and subordinates (for example, the superordinate might be *furniture* and the subordinate *chair*) or synonyms and antonyms, which may actually inhibit learning (*Now, which is left and which is right?*). A theme-based approach is, for the most part, better. That is, rather than trying to be exhaustive and teach all items in a set, those useful for the task are taught, so that *humid* and *airplane* may both be taught in the context of a unit on vacations (but not *dry* or *truck*).

Caution: While teaching vocabulary is important, doing so may lead some students to rely on plucking those words out of the text, and those words might not be the correct answers. Talking about wrong answers helps make students a little more sophisticated in their choice of listening strategies. Teaching synonyms may help too.

TABLE 10: Review of Keys to Pre-Teaching Vocabulary

- Make sure the words you teach are important to the task at hand.
- Worry about the context students will hear the words in. Don't try to teach all aspects of the meaning.
- Make sure students can recognize the pronunciation of the words.
- Label the pictures on the textbook page. Ask if anyone knows synonyms for those words.
- Write the topic of the listening in a circle. Draw lines outward from the circle. Solicit words that the students think of when they hear the topic. Keep branching out and adding new words.
- If you want students to remember the words, practice the next day and later. Multiple exposures are necessary.
- To review, play "odd one out." Write three words on the board. One is not related. Ask students to make a case for which words go together.
- To review, write the topic on the board, and ask teams of students to recall as many connected words as they can.

PRE-TEACHING GRAMMAR

You also might need to teach some grammatical structures that are frequent in the audio. Remember, though, you are teaching listening and not grammar. There is something very seductive about teaching grammar to language learners. They like it, and a lot of teachers like it (I love it). Again, remember the listening passage is likely to be short. Use planning time appropriately. Consider treating the grammar you think is important as lexical bundles or chunks of language. If you are doing a directions unit, *Turn left/right/at the light* is a useful structure for learners to be able to process. It might be useful to point out that this is a case where English does not use *please* (some languages do, and some learners transfer that use to English). It's doubtful, however, that students need a long lesson on the implied subject *you* in this structure.

TABLE 11: Reviews of Keys to Pre-Teaching Grammar

1. Teach the structures that are needed to understand the input. Ask yourself if any structures need to be taught at all.
2. Consider teaching structures as chunks of language, useful phrases.
3. Write the topic on the board. Ask students to brainstorm the sentences they are likely to hear.
4. During a second or third listening, focus on structures by having students raise their hands when they hear examples.
5. To review, have students construct dialogues from one-sentence examples of the structures or, given the topic again, brainstorm phrases or sentences associated with the topic.

3

Listening equals comprehension.

In the Real World . . .

One of the many joys of working for the University of Pittsburgh English Language Institute was working with new teachers. There was a strong classroom observation program in place, and we supervisors would visit classes several times a semester. I was the supervisor of speaking classes at the time and was sitting at the back of a basement classroom watching a new graduate assistant teach a lower-intermediate class. A student asked her, apropos of nothing in the lesson that I could see, "What does *cheat on* mean?" The teacher reddened and start to explain what she thought she heard—a much less polite term. The student had mispronounced two out of three of the sounds, and I could see what the teacher thought she heard, though I was pretty sure I heard *cheat*, which turned out to be the intended meaning. Perhaps I should have intervened, but people learn from difficult situations.

People mishear all the time. Children have limited vocabularies, and they fit what they hear into what they know. A child in John Irving's *The World According to Garp* (1978) is warned about the undertow in the ocean and imagines the Under Toad, a monster that

snatches swimmers. Sylvia Wright (1954) named these misunderstandings *mondegreens* after a line in a poem she heard as a child. The original was:

> They have slain the Earl Amurray
> And laid him on the green

She heard:

> They have slain the Earl Amurray
> And Lady Mondegreen

In other words, two homicides, not one. (Aren't old children's poems
strange?) Entire websites are dedicated to collecting mondegreens,
especially for rock lyrics. My point here is that listening is not all about
background knowledge. Other language skills—those we characterize
as bottom-up—are implicated in listening. This chapter and the next
address bottom-up skills.

What the Research Says . . .

For many years, almost since we began teaching listening, researchers
have made the distinction between teaching and testing, and many of
those researchers have criticized the dominant trend in listening
instruction as doing nothing to *teach* students how to listen. They
claimed that playing audio and asking comprehension questions, or
even playing audio and asking students to complete tasks, is merely
testing. In recent years, there have been challenges to what might be
called "the comprehension approach" to listening from several directions, the first concerned with teaching bottom-up skills in addition to
comprehension skills (for example, Field 2008a) and the second concerned with teaching strategy use, especially metacognitive strategy use
(for example, Goh 2008 and Vandergrift 2003a). A third position is

that of Jack Richards (2005), who notes that we have ignored activities "which require accurate recognition and recall of words, syntax and expression that occurred in the input" such as "dictation, cloze exercises, [and] identifying differences between a spoken and written text" (p. 87). Given our current knowledge of second language processes, Richards argues, we should have a second step in our listening classes, one that focuses on "listening as acquisition" (p. 90). After listening as comprehension, we should work with the input in written form (vocabulary, grammar, pronunciation) and utilize spoken activities like role plays and dialogues to help students acquire the language they have heard.

In this chapter, we will look at the first approach. We will continue the theme of bottom-up listening in the next chapter as well. For purposes of presentation, this chapter will concentrate on the processes involved in bottom-up listening, while the next organizes the material in terms of what makes listening difficult.

Bottom-Up Processing ———

Let's review the process that we use to listen. Conventionally, as we've seen, researchers talk about the process as consisting of decoding and comprehension (Wolff, 1987). Speech comes at the listener in an unbroken stream. To make sense of it, listeners must break that stream into groups of sounds, recognize the groups as words, recognize the meanings of the words, and understand how the words are related to each other. Listeners use their knowledge of the language, the world, and the immediate context to clear up the ambiguities. The immediate context, the conversation up to that point, sometimes called the "co-text" (Brown & Yule, 1983), helps the listener guess words in context and influences the interpretation of mispronounced words and words with multiple meanings.

Another element of decoding is parsing. Parsing means giving the words a grammatical meaning. In other words, the listener has to figure out who did what to whom. We listen first for meaning, which means that we don't explicitly focus on grammatical forms (VanPatten, 1996).

We aren't mentally diagramming sentences. However, there are clues listeners typically use to facilitate parsing. In English, we can assume a normal word order of SVO (subject-verb-object). We assume a single subject will agree with a single verb. We get information from pronouns; we know *he* is a do-er and *him* is the recipient of the action. There are other sources of information that don't rely on sentence grammar. "Animacy" is the quality of being a living thing; it helps us understand *The boy rode the bicycle,* because the bike riding the boy is outside our experience (MacWhinney, 2001). Finally, we intuitively understand that old information gets commented on by new. We have all these clues, as well as lexical ones like collocations (words reliably existing as a unit), pauses that serve to break the speech stream like commas break written text, and intonation, which can signal questions and statements. All these help us decode input. Because there are so many redundant signals, we actually do a fairly efficient job of decoding. To be sure, there are cases of ambiguity, like words with multiple meanings, but redundancy and context are usually able to quickly resolve any problems.

As I've said, for the past 30 years listening teachers have concentrated on building schemata, on the comprehension side of the equation. This is certainly important. In fact, again what we've done is adopt an analogy from reading research, Stanovich's Interactive Compensatory Hypothesis (1980). In this view, fluent listeners are able to process top-down, making use of world and contextual knowledge, until a breakdown in understanding necessitates the focused use of bottom-up resources, attention to individual sounds and words. Wolff saw this another way in 1987; his model said that top-down processing makes up for gaps in knowledge of the language. The first point is that the process is interactive. The second point is to draw attention to the use of the word *fluent.* In fact, fluent listeners need both top-down and bottom-up skills, and many of our students are not fluent listeners because they lack ability in bottom-up processing. They may, for example, have trouble segmenting the speech stream into words or not be able to efficiently and automatically recognize the words they know. Despite being poor at it, many beginning students choose bottom-up listening, word by word, as the way to make sense of input, probably because they believe understanding every word will lead to comprehension.

When you think about what it takes to understand a main idea, you can understand why a less-skilled listener would have a difficult time and retreat to more knowable individual words. Understanding a main idea involves integrating information from many parts of the text, while detail questions by definition ask for a smaller piece to be understood. Sometimes the answer can be matched directly to a word in the text. Of course, clever test makers may use this matching strategy against the test-taker.

This connection between less capable listeners and an over-reliance on bottom-up processing was the conclusion of Tsui and Fullilove (1998). In their analysis of seven years' worth of listening items on public English language achievement tests in Hong Kong, Tsui and Fullilove tried to discriminate the effects of schema type and question type on test scores. "Schema type" was divided into matching and non-matching. A matching schema type was one in which the schema activated remained valid throughout the input. A non-matching schema was one in which first, and then another, schema was activated on the basis of the input. Tsui and Fullilove (p. 440) give the example of an item that asked, "What saved the estate from burning down?" The passage first talked about the fire fighters (a possible answer) and only later talked about the wind direction, the correct answer. Question types were global (main ideas) and local (detail). Through analysis of the interaction between schema and questions, Tsui and Fullilove conclude that less-skilled listeners rely more on bottom-up listening.

Bottom-Up Listening: Characteristics of Spoken Text ———

We have said that the first step in listening is breaking up the speech stream. It's important to keep in mind that while words are broken apart on the page, making reading easier, there are no white spaces between words in speech. They all flow together, and it is the listener's task to break them apart in a meaningful way. This is made harder for language learners because they frequently learn dictionary forms of words, and so don't recognize them in speech when they change form or pronunciation (SIGnify vs. sigNIFicant). Words are also subject to assimilation, elision, and insertion, as well as the effects of weak forms (see Table 12). All these processes make comprehension difficult.

TABLE 12: Some Definitions for Phonological Processes

> **Assimilation:** a process in which a sound has an effect on a neighboring sound. For example, when spoken *ten men* sounds like *temmen* and *did you* sounds like *dijew.*
>
> **Elision (deletion):** a process in which a sound gets dropped, for example *every* when spoken sounds like *evry* and *family* sounds like *famly.*
>
> **Insertion:** a process by which a sound is added, often to break up two sounds that are difficult to pronounce. Consider the way some people say *athlete* as *athalete.*
>
> **Strong and weak forms (stressed and unstressed vowels):** In English, syllable strength/stress is important. Consider the word *open*, which has two syllables and two vowels. Like most English words, *open* is stressed on the first syllable (TA ta). The second syllable is unstressed; as a result, the *e* is a neutral sound formed in the middle of the mouth, a schwa, and sounds nothing like the *e* in the stressed syllable of *tell*. In fact, in rapid speech, the *e* in *open* is likely to disappear completely.

In addition to the phonological modifications that speech undergoes, there are effects on listening from accents, prosody (sentence stress and intonation), speech rate, pausing and hesitations, genres or discourse structure, and non-verbal signals like body language (see Table 13) . We will look at those later. This chapter will focus on how listeners recognize words in the speech stream.

TABLE 13: Important Characteristics of Spoken Texts

> **Phonological modification:** assimilation, elision, insertion, strong and weak forms
>
> **Accent:** known or unknown dialects of the target language
>
> **Prosody**: word stress, sentence stress, intonation
>
> **Speech rate:** fast or slow
>
> **Hesitation:** insertion of pauses or *um, ah,* etc.
>
> **Discourse features:** genres and features of genres
>
> **Non-verbal signals:** gestures, body language

Adapted from Buck, 2001.

Word Recognition ⎯⎯

Which words do learners process as they listen? Teachers frequently tell their students to listen for "key words," the most important words in the passage. According to Field (2008b), this is probably a good idea, or at least a realistic appraisal of what students do.

Words are frequently divided by grammarians into content words and function words. The concept of content word includes nouns, verbs, adjectives, and adverbs; in other words, words that carry lexical meaning. Function words are those that serve a grammatical function, such as prepositions, articles, or auxiliary verbs like *do, have,* and *be,* etc. While function words may lack lexical meaning, the fact that they are the glue of language makes them among the most frequently used and heard in English. However, they are not normally stressed within the sentence, unless we are contrasting them (Put it **in** the sink, not **next to** the sink). Field (2008b) was interested in the degree to which content and function words are processed. His study compared L1 English secondary students to English language learners at a private school in England. The learners had a variety of first languages and, while all were classified by the school as intermediate in level, differed slightly in proficiency. For the purposes of the study, they were divided into two groups, higher and lower proficiency. The native English speakers were also divided into two groups, based on their achievement in class.

Field's method was use of a paused transcript. Students listened to an interview that was paused after every four or five words; the students wrote what they heard. The better L1 English group was able to transcribe both content and function words effectively. The weaker L1 English group was slightly better able to accurately transcribe content words than function words. The two ELL groups transcribed the content words significantly better than the function words. Though the small number of students in each language group (the largest was 12 Spanish speakers) made statistical comparisons difficult, there appeared to be no effect for language. Even though German and Brazilian Portuguese behave somewhat similarly to English in terms of stress and rhythm, students with those native languages did not have an advantage. All language groups performed on average 20 percent lower on transcribing function words than content words, Italian speakers almost 30 percent lower. Furthermore, proficiency had an effect to the extent that higher-level students performed significantly better on both kinds of words, yet even those more advanced students had more trouble hearing function words. It is doubtless the case that native speakers of a language fill in the blanks. They use their knowledge of the language to "hear" things that aren't stressed. Proficient learners do this too. However, everyone is subject to confusion at times because function words are not stressed.

Of course, a listener may hear a content word perfectly well, but it might be an unknown word. When confronted with new words in the input, learners may completely ignore the context and the sound system and substitute a known word for an unknown one, even if it doesn't make much sense in the context or even if it's the wrong word class (a noun in a verb spot, for instance). These are the findings from a pilot study by Field (2004), who says this lexical effect may lie somewhere between the conventional notions of top-down and bottom-up processing. A psychological study by Broersma and Cutler (2008) looked at phantom word activation, essentially wrong guesses about words. Word boundaries may get incorrectly assigned (*a sister/assist her*) or a short word wrongly pulled out of a longer word (*me* out of *immediately*). Words may be misheard (*vocation/vacation*). Successful comprehension relies on suppressing the wrong guesses and choosing the right ones. Broersma and Cutler (2008) showed, however, that L2 listeners have a hard time suppressing non-words as quickly as we can in L1. Their subjects held on to their incorrect decisions longer in L2 than did an L1 control group. Broersma and Cutler concluded that even if students know a word, they may not be able to recognize it in speech and that the biggest problem in word recognition is probably distinguishing real words from non-words or near words. Learners may get stuck puzzling out misheard random collections of sound.

What strategies do listeners use to recognize words? Research suggests that phonological information is important. One important concept is phonotactics, which is concerned with the probabilities of sounds occurring at given places within words and sounds appearing together (consonant clusters, for example). In English, we can't begin a word with *nt*, but it's fine to end a word with it. Obviously, having this information allows one to segment speech because you understand where the word boundaries are, where one word begins and another ends. These aren't rules that are explicitly taught us in our L1; we acquire our understanding of them as a result of experience. We may, at least initially, transfer our L1 understanding of what is possible to L2, leading to problems. It does seem that highly proficient learners, who have a lot of experience with the L2, may in fact have knowledge of its phonotactics (Weber & Cutler, 2006).

Al-jasser (2008) tried to explicitly teach English phonotactics to Saudi Arabian undergraduate students of English in order to help them segment words. Success in training was measured by a word spotting task in which students had to find the word, press a button to measure their reaction time, and say the word. They were also measured by error rate, the number of times a word was missed. Words were classified as common boundary (same possibility for English and Arabic), (possible in) English boundary, (possible in) Arabic boundary, and no boundary (a combination not possible in either language). There were two groups, each of which received instruction in reductions, contractions, stress, and intonation in English. The control group transcribed 500 words of authentic English speech a week. The experimental group also received instruction in English phonotactics. This group was focused on pairings of consonants across words (*bw* and *dl* are possible initially in the dialect of Arabic the students spoke, but not in English, so English speakers know that it's *lab worker* and not *la bworker*). The experimental group did improve in reaction time and error rate, suggesting that explicit training in phonotactics may work. Of course, if you are teaching students whose language is similar to English in what combinations are possible, you would not bother. This is an issue for Arabic speakers, though.

Probabilities like phontactics are not the only way we know how to segment words. Another way that words get segmented in bottom-up processing, particularly in English, is through word stress. The vast majority of English words are either accented on the first syllable or monosyllabic, so the pattern is strong/weak (a troche, *Mary had a little lamb*). Thus, word stress helps segment words for native English speakers because each strong syllable is potentially the start of a new word. This is not true in other languages, and L2 listeners may use different cues; for example, French words are characteristically stressed weak/ strong (an iamb, *To be or not to be*), so French native speakers make more use of the syllable as a cue (Lynch, 1998). So far, the picture that is emerging is one of strong cue transfer from L1 to L2.

Field (2008c) says that students need to become aware that their comprehension is subject to revision, that their native processing strategies may lead them astray, and they need to question their understanding. Understanding needs to be constantly updated. Field's is a study based on a modified gating technique. Gating is a psychological research tool in which parts of an utterance are presented in syllables or time segments (gates), repeating the previous segment until the utterance is complete. In this case, Field presented an ambiguous two-syllable sequence divided into four gates. Students wrote what they heard at each gate, so their guesses could be tracked. The pattern (stressed, unstressed) could be a two-syllable word, two monosyllabic words, or a single syllable and the beginning of another word in English. First language English secondary students were compared to young adult French English learners and a mixed group, among which there were many Spanish native speakers. The greatest difference between the native English listeners and the non-native listeners was at the end. ELLs seemed reluctant to abandon their first segmentation hypothesis. We've also seen a reluctance for learners to abandon their word recognition guesses in Broersma and Cutler (2008). Field thinks this might have something to do with a lack of student confidence in listening abilities and says that when practicing segmentation in class, teachers should ask how certain learners are and why they are answering the way they are.

Tauroza (1993) suggested that students don't make much use of the ends of words. He asked 40 Italian university students of English to listen and complete a gapped transcript (fill in the blanks). They performed just as well in recognizing words when final consonants were not fully realized (assimilated, elided) as when they were. There seemed to be no problem in comprehension. Smith (2003) found that his Hong Kong students incorrectly transcribed song lyrics at the ends of words, which he took to be as a result of phonological differences between Cantonese and English. Conrad (1989) reported that Polish graduate students more accurately transcribed the first and last parts of English sentences.

Research by Zielinski (2008) suggests that listeners make use of their L1 listening strategies. Native listeners of Australian English did so when asked to transcribe English sentences spoken by speakers of Korean, Mandarin, and Vietnamese. The listeners relied heavily on syllable stress, initial consonants in segments, and stressed vowels (all important in English). Whenever the speakers gave a non-standard stress to a syllable, it caused comprehension difficulty because it didn't match expectations.

Reduced forms are another barrier to word recognition (Henrichsen, 1984). Teachers often teach reduced forms (*wanna* for *want to*) in pronunciation classes, probably most often for recognition. Brown and Hilferty (1986) investigated whether four weeks of daily lessons in recognition of reduced forms would help listening comprehension for Chinese students. The experimental group was explicitly taught the reduced forms and reviewed the forms periodically through dictations: teachers read the reduced form and students wrote the full form. A control group was taught minimal pairs (two words that differ in only one sound). Outcomes were measured by a grammar test, a listening comprehension test, and reduced form dictations. The experimental group outscored the control group on all measures, but only the scores on the grammar test and reduced forms dictation were statistically significantly different. Why the treatment had an effect on the grammar score is difficult to explain. Of course, the experimental group had practiced dictations throughout the course, so they might have been expected to do better on them, but the difference was not only significant, it was quite large. Finally, the researchers say that the lack of difference on the listening test may be attributed to the fact that very few reductions were used on the tape. It also may be the case that four weeks is not enough time to effect a change.

TABLE 14: Studies Relating to Word Recognition

L2 learners miss more function words than content words.	Field (2008b)
L2 learners substitute known words for unknown, can't suppress wrong choices.	Field (2004), Broersma & Cutler (2008)
Learners can learn L2 phonological processes.	Weber & Cutler (2006), Al-jasser (2008), Brown & Hilferty (1986)
Learners use L1 cues to segment words and process language.	Tauroza (1993), Lynch (1998), Smith (2003), Field (2008c), Zielinski (2008)

It's clear that listening is more than comprehension and top-down processing. This chapter has presented the processes that are implicated in dividing the speech stream into words and recognizing those words. These are clearly important abilities for students to have, and they are abilities that have not been stressed much in listening classes. Students need to work on moving away from their L1 default processing to L2 processing. The next section suggests some ways to help them do that, but I will make two general statements here:

- First, the role of the L1 is great in bottom-up listening difficulties. Having some knowledge of our students' L1s is helpful.
- Second, mistakes are often more helpful than correct answers if you use them as a window into listening processes. Talk through how students got the answers.

TABLE 15: Methodology: Measuring Decoding

Most of the studies in this chapter and most studies of bottom-up processing use psychological research methods, including measurements like reaction times. Some teachers have problems using studies like these because they often don't explicitly speak to the classroom. They don't have "ecological validity" because they are done in labs rather than the classroom (think of how many of the schema studies were classroom-based). My feeling is that we ought to get knowledge from anywhere we can, and think hard to apply it, but I see the objection. When we read studies, we have to ask ourselves not necessarily if the sorts of tasks that were done are the tasks that we use in the classroom, but what is at the core of the task, and how that relates to how we teach.

What We Can Do . . .

1. Work on knowledge of bottom-up processes.

The research on bottom-up listening shows word recognition and phonological processes like stress are important elements of decoding and, ultimately, comprehension. The prescription for better understanding bottom-up processes overall is not straightforward because it is a complex area and it's not clear that explicit teaching accomplishes as much as practice. But making students aware of how English is pronounced clearly focuses that practice. We are beginning to see a closer connection between listening and pronunciation in textbooks and in practice. For example, in our second edition of *Active Listening* (Brown

& Smith, 2007), we added an entire page of speaking activities at the end of each unit. The top of the page is a preview of the speaking activity, a pair work information or opinion exchange using the unit theme. The middle of the page uses phrases or sentences that learners will encounter in the pair work as examples in a pronunciation activity. The bottom of the page contains the prompt for the pair work. For example, the directions unit has students draw a map from their school to a nearby place and then explain the route to their partner who has to re-draw the map without looking at the original. The pronunciation task works on stress in choice questions: *Did you say **right** or **left**?* (Brown & Smith, 2007, p. 53). First, the learners listen and practice repeating choice questions and their answers (*Turn **right***). Then they look at some choice questions and circle the words they think will be stressed. Finally, they listen and check to see if they were correct. Now they are ready for the speaking activity.

In *English Firsthand* (Helgesen, Brown, & Wiltshier, 2010) we include a pronunciation activity (*Listen. Repeat silently. Then repeat out loud.*) for sentences students will use in the pair work activity in each unit. For the group work activity, there are also language models; the sentences have gaps. The students listen and fill in the blanks.

These sequences work on the principle that you have to be able to perceive a sound before you can produce it. That has been a given in pronunciation teaching for a long time, but we haven't always made an explicit connection between listening and pronunciation.

The popularity of minimal pair (two words differing by only one sound) practice has come and gone and come back again. Usually, learners are presented with two words and they have to say only Same (*bet/bet*) or Different (*bet/vet*). Then the teacher writes one sound under A [b] and another under B [v] and says a word containing that sound (*bet*); the students in this case answer A.

Beyond understanding individual sounds, listeners also must be able to segment the stream of speech they hear into recognizable words. Working with stress and intonation helps this understanding. The majority of English words are stressed on the first syllable, and impor-tant, information-carrying words are the stressed words in sentences.

Stress contributes to intonation; statements and different kinds of questions have predictable intonation patterns. Students can work with transcripts to mark the stressed words or syllables as they listen, or they can write down the stressed words they hear.

Listeners also need to be able to break the stream into thought groups. Speakers pause and group words into ideas. We see this in writing when writers use commas and periods, but it is no less a feature of speech. Learners can work with transcripts to predict where the pauses are (based on meaning), put slashes between the thought groups, and then listen and check.

Listeners have a difficult time understanding reduced speech (*Whaddaya* for *What do you* and *wanna* for *want to*). Students can listen to examples of reduced speech (the teacher can dictate) and then write the full form. They can also use a script with words missing, predict what the words would be based on meaning and grammar, and fill in the blanks while listening. See Celce-Murcia, Brinton, Goodwin, & Griner (2010) for an overview of pronunciation teaching. Gilbert (1995) is a good source for teaching techniques that focus on stress and intonation.

Dictation is also a useful tool. I will have more to say about dictation in Myth 5.

TABLE 16: Review of Practicing Bottom-Up Processes in Listening

1. **Transcriptions and dictations**
2. **Chunking:** Divide a transcript into meaningful chunks while listening. Take advantage of pauses to notice the chunks. Later, predict chunks and listen to confirm.
3. **Phonemic contrasts:** Answer A or B to discriminate minimal pairs.
4. **Grouping:** Match sounds or stresses in columns. Give examples in columns, and dictate words that are similar in either sounds or stress patterns.
5. **Fill in the blanks in transcripts:** Use phrases rather than individual words.
6. **Dictate reduced forms:** Students write the full form.
7. **Add a physical element:** Students tap out or clap the stresses in a sentence or word. Students mime the rise or fall of sentences.

2. Don't forget vocabulary.

We need to spend more time on teaching vocabulary. Then spend time reviewing the vocabulary we've taught, so that students know more next time. A favorite teacher complaint is, "I taught it, but they didn't learn it." With vocabulary, you need to give students the chance to encounter the word at least a dozen times, in non-trivial, focused ways. We really have had too much faith in "guessing from context." We need to bring vocabulary back into all language classrooms (see Folse, 2004, for extensive coverage of this research). In the new edition of *English Firsthand* (Helgesen, Brown, & Wiltshier, 2010) we added a whole-page picture dictionary as the first page of each unit; it previews the words in the unit. We then obviously use those words and give opportunities to review them.

The most important thing that students need to know about a word if they are to use it in listening is its aural realization—how it sounds. We also need to teach the various forms of the word beyond the dictionary form because that's not the form they are most likely to hear. As this chapter has shown, stress is important. When teaching vocabulary, we need to consider this. One way is to dictate words and have students place them in columns under words that have similar stress patterns.

3. Use tasks, not comprehension questions.

This piece of advice wasn't in my original plan. I had assumed we don't do this anymore. Every listening textbook I've seen in the past several years has gotten away from asking comprehension questions at the same time they have stayed focused on comprehension itself. But then I thought of all the listening tests out there, and I thought about the comprehension questions that accompany the readings in writing text-books I've used. So maybe this topic does need addressing, particularly if you are thinking of writing your own materials.

The main issue here is teaching versus testing. Historically, listening classes didn't always make the distinction. Testing tries to weed people out, and, at its worst, can be tricky. Teaching tries to support the students in their task so that they perform that task better in the future. If we play a piece of audio, and then ask questions like, "What time will the train arrive?" we don't take advantage of what students already know. No, they won't know what time the train is scheduled to arrive in this particular piece of audio, but if we ask them the question *before* they listen, they are listening for a more limited range of information. They know the possibilities, hour plus minutes. This is incidentally a very basic test-taking strategy that my students don't always think about: read the questions first, and then read the reading passage or listen to the audio. So, if you are preparing materials and want to teach students how to listen more effectively, ask the questions first. There is some research on this point in the testing field. Yanagawa and Green (2008) looked at performance on multiple choice tests in three conditions: one in which both the question stem and answer options were on the page, one in which the answers were concealed and the question written, and one in which the answer options were on the test paper, but the question was on the audio. Though the first two conditions had equal results, the last led to decreased comprehension. So, seeing the answers is not necessarily the most important thing—seeing the question is.

4

Because L1 listening ability is effortlessly acquired, L2 listening ability is, too.

In the Real World . . .

My Vienna story in Myth 2 showed that sometimes you don't need to understand much of a transaction in order to participate effectively. In my case, I literally understood nothing and still got what I wanted.

Anyone who has studied a language understands the haze a beginning learner often is in. What many beginners do is grab a piece of a conversation and run with it. You can make yourself seem quite competent by being able to pick out the word *drink* from the question, *Sir, I wonder if you'd like anything more to drink.* You might have no idea what some of the rest of the words mean and may not be able to construct that same sentence yourself, but you can get another glass of tea. As we've seen, part of your competence is that you are sitting at a café or restaurant, and you are reasonably sure that the server is not asking you for the time of day. Another thing that makes this easy is the fact you are using transactional language; you are getting something done.

For example, on the same European trip, I was trying to buy train tickets from Madrid to Lisbon. I asked the clerk for two tickets and was greeted by a torrent of Spanish that included the word *huelga*, which I knew means *strike*. I realized there had been a strike called that morning and that we were going nowhere. In that case, I couldn't have predicted the situation, and in fact would have expected the follow-up question to be about class of travel or time of departure. Picking one word out of many led to understanding, but I was lucky. It could have been a word I didn't know.

Relying on a word here and there doesn't always work. In fact, we need lots—and lots—of words. I'm sure we've all had the experience of not being as successful in an unpredictable interactional situation, such as a conversation, as we are in transactional situations, like buying tickets. Many beginners have been embarrassed by a direct question from a conversational partner they have been nodding to, but not really understanding. In that situation, it may be that there are so many unknown words and the conversation may twist so that neither context nor individual words help.

As we've seen in previous chapters, part of the reason the comprehension approach to listening has been popular is a belief that listening is easily acquired through practice. We've said that's definitely part of the story, but that we need to shine light on other aspects of the listening process, too. This chapter will extend Myth 3 and will remain focused for the most part on "the little things" of listening like vocabulary, speech rate, accent, and individual differences. We will place them in the context of what makes listening difficult and expand the discussion into one larger thing, pragmatic comprehension.

What the Research Says . . .

Learners and Their Perceived Problems in Listening ——

"The little things" show up as problems over and over again in what is an active line of research on what learners find difficult in listening. This research usually takes the form of questionnaires, which are sometimes followed up with interviews.

An early questionnaire-based study of Hong Kong students and teachers (Boyle 1984) reported that students stressed the contribution of vocabulary to listening comprehension much more than teachers did. Other factors mentioned by students and virtually ignored by teachers were memory and attention or concentration. Some students speculated that reading habits and listening comprehension were linked. Teachers stressed speaker clarity, the immediate acoustical environment (noise, interference), and motivation. Both groups put practice opportunities at the top of their lists of important factors affecting listening comprehension.

One study that combined a relatively large number of questionnaires (given to 595 high school learners of French in England) and interviews (with 28 students) found that many students believed they were just not any good at listening. They were skeptical that anything could help them, though some of the students said they used a strategy of listening to what they perceived to be key words in the text. Unfortunately, the researcher points out, key words were "words they recognized, which might or might not be important for understanding the text" (Graham, 2006, p. 177).

Learners perceived that their problems in comprehension stemmed from "speed of delivery of texts, making out individual words in a stream of spoken French, and making sense of any words that have been identified or understood" (Graham, 2006, p. 178).

Graham's results echo those of Goh (2000), who also used a combination of questionnaires and interviews, including group and individual interviews of Chinese students studying English in Singapore.

Goh enumerated ten problems, five of which were due to word recognition and attention failure (p. 59). Students

- failed to recognize words they knew
- got stuck thinking about a word and thereby lost the rest of the input
- couldn't break the stream of language into proper chunks
- missed the beginning of texts
- either concentrated too hard or failed to concentrate

Students also had five other problems, most of which revolved around an inability to put the words they understood into a form they could use. They could see the trees, but couldn't put together a conception of a forest. When Goh compared higher- and lower-ability students, she found they shared difficulties with word recognition and forgetting what they'd heard; the high-ability group understood more words and still couldn't form a general meaning, while the lower-ability group was more likely to get lost thinking about meanings of unknown, or partly known, words.

Both studies confirmed research done by Flowerdew and Miller (1992, 1996) on the perceived (lecture) listening problems of Hong Kong university students. The first study surveyed student opinions, while the second surveyed teacher opinions. Both saw problems in comprehension resulting from speed of delivery, vocabulary knowledge, and difficulties in concentrating (some of the lectures were two hours long). Lecturers also believed that comprehension could be improved by providing more examples of and context for the information. Flowerdew, Miller, and Li (2000) extended their research to classes taught by Chinese lecturers in English; in these classes as well, speed of delivery and lack of vocabulary knowledge, especially knowledge of specialist vocabulary, led to problems in comprehension.

Confirmation of these studies was found in an L1 Arabic EFL situation by Hasan (2000). Learners saw their difficulties in listening as being vocabulary, grammatical structures, and text length (p. 142).

They also had problems with the speed of delivery, hesitations, and pauses of natural speech, as well as problems with different accents of English (p. 146). Furthermore, students admitted they found it difficult to understand texts if they weren't interested in the topic (p. 148). This suggests the role of motivation in listening.

It seems to me this research beautifully sums up the interactive nature of listening. Though students report that they have significant perceptual problems with breaking the speech stream into recognizable words, many also report that forming a main idea (a top-down process) is difficult. Remember that the main idea is not the finished product we might think. It's not the answer to a comprehension question, but more of an on-going representation that listeners hold (and change) as new information comes in.

The studies reported were concerned with student and faculty perceptions of difficulty as measured by questionnaires and interviews. In Wu (1998), we have a retrospective study of learner difficulties on a standardized test. Six intermediate ELLs with L1 Chinese listened to a short radio interview from a retired version of a test of English proficiency and answered six multiple choice questions. Then they explained their answers to the researcher, in English. The input was an interview with someone who was in a rock band in his youth.

Wu concludes that the listeners made use of their general schematic knowledge when their knowledge of the language failed them. They often did so by latching onto a stressed word in the input. For example, the student coded BL got the correct answer for the wrong reasons by applying this strategy. She heard *exciting* and guessed based on two faulty assumptions: *exciting* is not related to *relaxing* and traditional music isn't exciting. Those assumptions led her to dismiss two possible answers, leaving her with what she (wrongly) thought was a 50/50 chance at the correct answer. The student coded CQ heard *attitude* and matched it with an incorrect answer. Sometimes, however, knowledge of the topic made the students choose an incorrect answer, as when the presence of *fashion* (meaning *way*) in an answer led three students to choose it, based on their association of rock music and clothing.

Students had trouble segmenting the speech stream. BL heard "was our manager's idea" as "without manager's idea." They also had trouble with vocabulary, such as *tolerate* and *put up with*. Indeed, the most reported problem in listening comprehension was vocabulary knowledge.

TABLE 17: Studies Related to Perceived Problems in Listening

Vocabulary	Boyle (1984), Flowerdew & Miller (1992), Flowerdew, Miller & Li (1996), Hasan (2000), Goh (2000), Graham (2006)
Memory/attention/ concentration	Boyle (1984), Flowerdew & Miller (1992), Goh (2000)
Motivation	Boyle (1984), Hasan (2000)
Speed of delivery	Flowerdew & Miller (1992), Flowerdew, Miller & Li (1996), Hasan (2000), Graham (2006)
Acoustical environment (is this an aspect of attention/concentration?)	Boyle (1984)
Few practice opportunities	Boyle (1984)
Segmenting speech	Graham (2006)
Main idea	Goh (2000)
Grammatical structures	Hasan (2000)
Text length (is this also an aspect of attention/concentration?)	Hasan (2000)
Hesitations, pauses	Hasan (2000)
Accents	Hasan (2000)

The Role of Vocabulary in Listening Comprehension ——

We mentioned pre-teaching vocabulary earlier. Here I want to focus on a number of studies that have looked at the role of vocabulary in the process of listening comprehension. Folse (2004) has argued for the primary importance of vocabulary in overall language development, and Vandergrift (2006) has argued for a larger role for vocabulary in listening development, specifically.

I've found that teachers are very interested in knowing the number of words that students need for proficiency in English. First of all, we have to define what it means to know a word. In terms of listening, we might consider receptive vocabulary (recognizing a word) rather than productive (being able to use the word). Knowledge of a word's pronunciation is very important in listening. There are many such issues concerning what it means to know a word that we needn't concern ourselves with at this point. More important, as Nation (2006) points out, we need to address learner goals when thinking about how many words they need. Students could try to learn all the words in English, but nobody knows all the words in any language. Another way to look at the question is to ask how many words a native speaker of English knows. A figure of 20,000 for an educated adult has been suggested, but Nation (p. 60) thinks that might be too high a number. A final way to approach this question is to look at how students will use the words, in what situations, and with which materials. Nation used the British National Corpus, a collection of 100 million words of mostly written text (90 percent written, 10 percent spoken) to investigate vocabulary sizes for reading and listening. A corpus can be ordered by frequency, and corpora are often divided into thousand-word frequency bands. Thus, researchers can talk about text coverage in thousand-word increments: this book can be read by someone who knows 2,000, 3,000, 4,000, 5,000 word families, etc. (A word family includes a word's grammatical inflections and derivational suffixes. For example, *walk, walks, walked, walker,* etc. is one word family).

Nation (2006) first looked at how many words would be needed to be familiar with most of the words in a children's movie, *Shrek.* Of course, movies provide visual context, so some meanings can be inferred, but Nation says that a knowledge of 4,000 word families (plus proper nouns) provide almost 97 percent of coverage. The script itself is about 10,000 words long and uses only about 1,100 word families, but those families are strung across the 4,000 most common words. The idea of vocabulary size indicates that we cannot predict the exact words that are needed, so it's most useful to look at bands of word families. Thus, if non-native speakers of English knew the 4,000 most common words of

English in the BNC, they would have a good chance of understanding the movie (there would be one unknown word in every 30). With a vocabulary of the 7,000 most common word families, the viewer would have to cope with only one unknown word per 50.

Two sections of the Wellington Corpus of Spoken English were used to investigate how many words are needed to cope with unplanned spoken English (Nation, 2006). The sections were transcripts of talk radio and conversations between friends and family. Nation found that 3,000 word families, plus proper nouns, would provide 95 percent coverage of the material in the corpus (but this would mean about seven unknown words per minute), and 6,000–7,000 word families would provide 98 percent coverage. Thus, Nation finally recommended a 6,000–7,000 word vocabulary for listening to conversations. Of course, words that are unknown in the beginning of the input may become known through repetition and context, though probably not acquired, unless the repetition is very frequent. Speech uses a lot of the most frequent words in the language (perhaps as much as 85 percent of a conversation is built solely on very common words), so listeners are at some advantage, compared to readers, but the fleeting nature of speech imposes other burdens on the listener, as we have seen. Adolphs and Schmitt (2003), in an analysis based on CANCODE (Cambridge and Nottingham Corpus of Discourse in English), said that 5,000 word families would reach about 96 percent of conversational English.

These studies focused on vocabulary breadth. Staehr (2009) investigated the role of vocabulary breadth and depth on listening comprehension. Breadth of vocabulary is the number of words that a learner has some knowledge of. Depth is a measure of how well or connected the words are; it is often tested by the Word Associates Test (Read, 2000). Staehr gives the example of *fluctuate* from the Word Associates Test. The three correct answers (out of eight) are *irregular, rates,* and *vary.*

Staehr tested 115 Danish university EFL learners; the students were upper intermediate, and 40 percent of them had lived for at least five months in an English-speaking country. Vocabulary size and depth were both significantly correlated with scores on a standardized listening comprehension test. Vocabulary size had a correlation of .70, and depth had a correlation of .65, both relatively strong and, in terms of statistical difference, the same strength. Together, they predict half the variance (51 percent) in the listening scores, meaning that 49 percent of the scores are the result of something else. However, when Staehr did further analysis, he found that it was vocabulary size that was making by far the greatest contribution to the results (49 percent of the variance), while depth added only another 2 percent. Of course, it is difficult to separate the two in reality, since each is correlated strongly to the other. In a separate analysis, Staehr endorses the 5,000 most frequent word families as a good target for listening comprehension.

Kelly (1991) flatly states that lack of vocabulary knowledge is the main reason advanced foreign language listeners have difficulties in comprehension. Kelly has two data sets, one the first 100 errors in the transcription of a BBC radio newscast by an L1 French teacher of L2 English and the other a set of errors made in BBC transcriptions by 38 Francophone students. The students transcribed and translated the broadcasts; errors made by at least 20 percent of the students were analyzed.

In the teacher's case, 45 of the hundred errors were perceptual. Kelly admits that a native speaker could have made many of the same mistakes, for example *increasing* for *increase in*, *has been* for *is being*, and *the* for *a*. Others could also be made by native speakers who were asked to repeat what they just heard, as with *everybody/everyone* and *workmen/workers*. Others were due to phonological transfer of French to English (*Henderson/Anderson*, *in sight/inside*). Of the lexical errors, many simply reflected a cultural or general knowledge gap, such as *Ennis/NS* road service station and *run/Rand* Daily Mail. Some lexical errors involved ignorance of collocation (*over a large/long* period of time) and syntactic errors (*prior to/apart of* these two meetings).

The students had five to seven years of English study, so they were less advanced than the teacher. Compared to the teacher, the learners made a much smaller percentage of perceptual errors and a much larger percentage of lexical errors. Learners made what might be characterized as broader errors: *the thing I hate most/the thing I A most; and if you're stuck in/and if your studies are*. The clear distinction Kelly frequently makes between perceptual and lexical errors ultimately, however, is a line that's difficult to draw, given that perception and word recognition are intertwined. His methods of transcribing and translating are also unorthodox. However, his point that more vocabulary instruction is needed is well taken .

More convincing is the study of Bonk (2000), which tested Japanese university English learners on four pieces of audio with increasing lexical difficulty. Overall, there was a moderate positive correlation (.446) between lexical knowledge and comprehension scores on a recall measure. The more vocabulary knowledge, the more was understood. However, students showed individual differences. While it was not likely that high comprehension would occur with low lexical scores, some students scored as low as 60 percent on the vocabulary test and still attained good comprehension, probably because they used compensatory strategies effectively.

Mecartty (2000) added the variable of grammatical knowledge to that of lexical knowledge. The study looked at the effects of both kinds of knowledge on both reading and listening comprehension. The subjects were 154 American college students in their final semester of a four-semester Spanish sequence. Vocabulary knowledge was measured by translation and antonym tasks, while grammatical knowledge was measured by multiple choice sentence completion and grammaticality judgment tasks. The reading and listening groups both read/heard the same text, but in the case of the listening group the text was read in a way that simulated a radio broadcast feature. Comprehension was measured by a multiple choice test of main ideas and details. Both lexical and grammatical knowledge were important to comprehension, but only lexical knowledge significantly correlated to both listening and reading comprehension. Lexical knowledge explained more of the variance in reading, meaning it was more important to reading. In listening, there are apparently other factors involved, though the experiment was not designed to say which they were. Mecartty concludes that someone with a good vocabulary will probably be successful at reading and listening, but the same can't be said of someone with a high degree of grammatical knowledge.

When does vocabulary have to be taught? To remind you of schema studies, Berne (1995), Elkhafaifi (2005a), and Chang and Read (2006) found that immediate vocabulary instruction (prior to the listening task) had no significant facilitative effects on comprehension. Chang (2007) studied the effects of timing on vocabulary instruction in classes of Taiwanese EFL learners. There were three groups. One group was given a 25-word vocabulary list one week before a test, another the day before, and the third the day of the test (they studied the list for 30 minutes). Students were told that the words would be included in the aural text of the test. They were given a vocabulary test, a listening comprehension test, and a post-test questionnaire. A subset of students was interviewed. Results showed that length of time had an effect on vocabulary scores, but not on listening scores. (Of course, Chang didn't know if or for how long students actually studied the words.) In the interviews, it became clear that members of the first two groups made no effort to pronounce the words as part of their preparation, while most members of the third group did try to practice the pronunciation of the words. Chang speculates that this might have helped these students attain scores as good as the others who had an opportunity to study longer because in listening the oral form of the word is, of course, very important.

Mixed findings about the role of vocabulary in listening comprehension were found in Mehrpour and Rahimi (2010), who also looked at reading comprehension. Their students were studying EFL at a university in Iran. Mehrpour and Rahimi investigated general vocabulary knowledge as well as specific or key words found in the texts. While there were no effects for general vocabulary knowledge on listening comprehension, providing specific key words before the test increased performance on the listening test, though not by much. Previewing vocabulary had a bigger effect on reading comprehension. The researchers claim that listening comprehension is not assisted in the same way as reading because standardized listening tests, though they ask for recall of specific information, rarely require listeners to know the exact words of the text, whereas reading tests often do rely on the meanings of specific words.

I think what all of these studies show is that it is somewhat unrealistic to teach a word once and expect students to retain it for use. Even if students have immediate access to glosses of the words, as they had in Mehrpour and Rahimi's study, there is just simply too much going on, too many demands placed on the listener, and no time for a listener to consult the glossary. It is better to adopt a program of vocabulary learning based on word frequencies that allows students to encounter the words sufficiently frequently and in enough varied contexts to allow for their automatic use. With an adequate vocabulary base, pre-teaching vocabulary then becomes a matter of activation of known words or quick teaching of uncommon words crucial to understanding.

Speech Rate and Listening Comprehension ——

It's common sense that utterances spoken quickly are more difficult to understand than utterances spoken slowly. There's less time to segment the speech stream and recognize vocabulary. Articulation suffers, and words lose their shapes. At bottom, speech rate is both idiosyncratic and subject to change based on situations. When we speak formally, we tend to slow down. When excited, we tend to speed up. So, in a sense there are so many variables that instruction doesn't influence. What most teachers try to do is gradually adjust speech rates as students increase in proficiency, but it's all a matter of feel. *Foreigner talk* (see Chaudron, 1988, for a review) is the name given to speech adjusted in many ways to increase comprehension in non-native speakers of a language. Speech is typically slowed, redundancy is built in with restatements and synonyms, simple words are used, and non-verbal signals like pointing may increase. The analogy is often made to the way caregivers speak to children learning their first language. There has been some debate over the years as to what part of foreigner talk is most useful to the listener, and many would say that speech rate is not the most important component. Nevertheless, because it was named by students in several studies as a significant factor in listening comprehension and because teachers are often interested in this too, I will next present several studies on optimal speech rates for listening.

The first thing that strikes anyone looking into the literature on speech rate is that everybody uses a different description of *fast* and *slow.* An often-quoted baseline is Tauroza and Allison (1990), who report the average speech rate of British English as 230–280 words per minute (wpm) or 3.8–4.7 syllables per second (sps). This number surfaces again in research by Derwing and Munro (2001), who found that L1 Mandarin advanced learners of English preferred the same speech rate for Mandarin-accented and Canadian-accented English, 4.5 sps. A mixed-language group of advanced L2 English speakers preferred that the Mandarin-accented English be spoken at a slightly slower rate than Canadian-accented English (4.1 sps to 4.3 sps). Overall, of course, there were individual differences in preferences.

Griffiths (1990) claims that speech faster than 200 wpm (which he equates to 3.8 sps) impairs comprehension for lower-level learners. In his study, a rate of 100 wpm was more easily comprehended than a rate of 200 wpm, but comprehension at 100 wpm was not better than 150 wpm. In a second study (Griffiths, 1992), Omani teachers-in-training heard stories at 5 sps, 3.75 sps, and 2.5 sps and then answered 15 true or false questions. The slowest speed led to highest comprehension, but the average and highest speech rates did not lead to significantly different results. This basically replicates his finding that 200 wpm is a barrier to understanding. Zhao (1997) found that students who had the ability to control speech rate and repeat the text comprehended better than those without the opportunity. Of the 15 subjects in the study who could slow the speech, 14 did. Zhao's method of allowing student control is a perhaps a good idea for training sessions, but of course we can't ultimately control the speech rate of others. Probably the best we can do is teach students to ask their interlocutors to slow down, but that usually only works for a limited time.

Speech rate interacts with a number of factors, including accent and attitudes toward the speaker. Anderson-Hsieh and Koehler (1988) took into account all three factors as they tested the comprehension by native speakers of English (university undergraduates) to three native speakers of Chinese with varying degrees of proficiency. The students also listened to a native speaker of English from Iowa as a control. The speakers read passages at various speeds. The slow rate was 2.39–2.65 sps, the regular rate was 3.25–3.49 sps, and the fast rate was 4.22–4.58 sps. Subjects took a comprehension test based on each passage and answered questionnaires about their attitudes toward foreigners and accented speech. Anderson-Hsieh and Koehler report that comprehension scores were lower for the Chinese speakers than for the Iowa speaker, and the scores corresponded to the degree of accentedness (the most proficient nonnative speaker was the easiest for the undergraduates to understand). Fast speech was more difficult to understand than slow speech, though there was no difference between regular and slow. That's probably all to be expected, as is the finding that those with a more favorable view of foreigners did better when speech was faster and accent was greatest (because they did not dismiss the speaker out of hand). Attitude does play a part in how we understand. One other interesting aspect of the study was that prosody was more important to understanding than individual sounds were, which supports the views of pronunciation teachers who work more on stress and intonation than on individual sounds.

In a study of the effects of rate reduction and exact repetition, Jensen and Vinther (2003) hypothesized that an immediate verbatim repetition of input would allow learners to process form, after having processed meaning the first time, which, remember from Myth 3, is what we do. They also manipulated the speed of the input. Their subjects were second-year Danish university students learning Spanish. Two versions of videotaped dialogues were prepared, one at the original speed and one a slowed version (there was no report on exact speeds). The video was segmented to allow for repetition of fragments. Two experimental groups listened to the repetitions at different speeds, either fast-slow-fast or fast-slow-slow. Results were measured by elicited imitation, by which the subjects, immediately after hearing the fragments, had to reproduce as exactly as possible the content they had heard, including all the false starts. They were scored on gains (from pre-test to post-test) on global comprehension, phonological decoding, and grammatical accuracy of selected forms. Both experimental groups improved significantly compared to the control group on all three measures. The scores showed no advantage for either speed pattern. A second study tried to separate the repetition and speed factors. The fast-fast-fast group had slightly higher scores on comprehension and phonological decoding, but slightly lower scores on grammatical accuracy. In questionnaires that asked for student reactions, the chance to hear input again was understandably popular. A few members of the fast-fast-fast group reported that if they hadn't understood the fragments the first two times, the third was useless. Others said it was difficult to maintain concentration on the three fast listenings. The work of Jensen and Vinther seems to contradict that of Zhao in the sense that repetition was more important that speed.

Blau (1990) added the effects of syntax and pausing to the investigation of speech rates. In Blau's first experiment, groups drawn from ELLs in Poland and Puerto Rico heard simple and complex sentences at speeds of 145 wpm (slow) and 170 wpm (fast). There were no significant differences in comprehension scores. Blau contrasted the effects of pausing and speed in the second experiment. One group heard texts at 200 wpm, another at 185 wpm, and a third at 185 wpm with pauses inserted at approximately 23-word intervals. The group that heard the paused texts scored significantly higher on comprehension. The slowed version actually yielded the lowest scores, except for the very lowest-level students in Puerto Rico.

Though pausing, particularly carefully designed pausing, is an effective tool for increasing comprehension, the normal hesitations of everyday speech sometimes present a challenge to listeners. Twenty-two German learners of English transcribed spontaneous speech from audio (Voss, 1979). The text had a number of examples of hesitations such as repeats, false starts (self-interruptions), filled pauses (*er, uh*), and unfilled pauses (silence or lengthened syllables). Though students made a number of errors transcribing the material, almost one-third of their errors resulted at places where there were hesitations. The problems fell into two categories. In the first, students misunderstood repetition or filled pauses for words or parts of words (the false start *in say, in technical* was transcribed as *same Technical, santenical, saying technical*). In the second, words or parts of words were mistaken for repetition or filled pauses (*one of the problems—erm—of people who work* transcribed as *one of the problems people who work*). Voss recommends use of authentic speech in the classroom to get students used to the natural phenomenon of hesitations.

Simplified and Elaborated Input ——

In addition to slowing down and adding pauses, teachers and others speaking to language learners often modify their input or change their speech in one of two other ways. They simplify (pare down) or elaborate (repeat and paraphrase) (Ehrlich, Avery, & Yorio, 1989). Which is better for comprehension? Long and Ross (1993) surveyed ten studies, a number of them unpublished, and found that both simplification and elaboration were effective. Furthermore, there was some evidence that either type of modification was more effective in helping lower proficiency students than higher.

Are some kinds of restatements better than others? Chaudron (1983) compared a number of possibilities and found that repeating the noun, the subject of a sentence, was most effective. Derwing (1996) asked two questions: What kind of paraphrase is effective? How does too much elaboration affect listeners? Marked paraphrase, such as the use of phrases like *in other words*, unmarked paraphrase (present but no attention drawn to it), and irrelevant detail were compared to an unmodified baseline. In a drawing task in which one student had to reproduce the picture of the other without seeing it, pairs of native speakers of English did best with marked paraphrase and worst with the baseline and irrelevant detail. English language learners did worst with irrelevant detail, and their results in two of the three trials were the same for marked and unmarked paraphrase; they didn't attend to the markers. Subjects in the third gave very few correct answers, so it's difficult to draw conclusions from that study. Overall, paraphrase was the most effective in aiding comprehension, but irrelevant details hurt comprehension, confirming the suggestions of Chiang and Dunkel (1992). The results also confirm Ehrlich, Avery, & Yorio, 1989) who found that "embroidery" (excessive elaboration) led to a lower rate of task success than "skeletonizing" (simplification) in an information gap task in which native speakers of English were the speakers and English learners the listeners.

TABLE 18: Studies on Improving Listening Comprehension

Increased redundancy and repetition facilitates comprehension	Chaudron (1983) Pica, Young, & Doughty (1987): more effective than simplification Chiang & Dunkel (1992): redundancy only helped higher proficiency learners Cervantes & Gainer (1992) Derwing (1996): relevant elaborations help, while extraneous detail harms Jensen & Vinther (2003)
Decreased rate of speech facilitates comprehension	Kelch (1985): decreased rate of speech more effective than modifying input Blau (1990): decreased rate effective at lower proficiency levels Griffiths (1992) Zhao (1997) Derwing & Munro (2001): no need to decrease rate for advanced learners Jensen & Vinther (2003): repetition at same or lower rates increased comprehension
Simplified syntax facilitates comprehension	Ehrlich, Avery, & Yorio (1989): better than excessive elaboration Blau (1990): no effect for simplified syntax in listening Cervantes & Gainer (1992)
Insertion of pauses facilitates comprehension	Blau (1990) Lesser (2004): helps with unfamiliar topics

Accent and Intelligibility ⸺

Accent is another factor in listening comprehension. Accent has traditionally been measured by what Levis (2005) calls "the nativeness principle." The goal of pronunciation teaching until recently was to make students sound native-like. The nativeness principle contrasts with "the intelligibility principle," in which the goal is to make students understood by all of their listeners.

A line of research that studies intelligibility judgments has thus opened up. Researchers have been interested for some years in whether people tend to understand each other better when they have similar language backgrounds or if familiarity with the accent is sufficient

(Flowerdew, 1994). Tauroza and Luk (1997) argued that previous research suffered methodological flaws. In their study, 63 Hong Kong secondary students, native speakers of Cantonese, listened to short stories read by "typical" speakers of two dialects, British English RP (the most prestigious British dialect) and Hong Kong English. The typical speakers were chosen from eight total speakers; subjects had judged them most typical. The two speakers recorded one story each, and students in two classes listened twice, wrote recalls, and answered questions on a multiple choice test. Students scored higher on both tests after listening to the RP speaker, but the difference was not statistically significant. Moreover, the class that listened to the Hong Kong accent was slightly more proficient at the time of the last listening assessment, and the Hong Kong speaker spoke slower than the RP speaker. This should have given an advantage to the group that heard the Hong Kong speaker, but the results were in fact basically the same. This leads Tauroza and Luk to conclude that there is no same-accent advantage in listening.

Bent and Bradlow (2003) come to a slightly different conclusion. They claim an "interlanguage speech intelligibility benefit." In their study, monolingual English speakers understood each other better than they understood non-native speakers of English whose L1s were Chinese and Korean. However, for the non-native listeners (L1 Chinese, L1 Korean, and a mixed group with several different L1s), intelligibility of highly proficient learners from the same language background was equal to that of the English speakers. Furthermore, intelligibility of highly proficient non-native speakers from a different background was greater than or equal to the intelligibility of the English speakers. Bent and Bradlow do point out that there were large individual differences among the scores.

Given that most people who use English as an auxiliary language are talking to others who, like themselves, are not native speakers, and given the wide variety of Englishes in the world, listening assessment as a field needs to understand who the speakers in the test input should be. Major and his colleagues (2002) recorded lectures in English by speakers of Chinese, Japanese, Spanish, and Standard American

English and then tested the listeners' comprehension. Only the L1 Spanish listeners had an advantage listening to someone who shared their first language. Chinese students listening to Chinese speakers lecturing in English actually scored lower than they did listening to the other speakers. Chinese and Japanese scored equally well listening to Standard American English and L1 Spanish speakers. The researchers speculate that the advantage may be a result of the fact that Chinese and Japanese are more similar in their rhythms to Spanish than English. The three languages share syllables of relatively equal length and very little vowel reduction. Of course, attitudes play a large role in judgments of the intelligibility of others, and the researchers say that might have been a factor.

A second study by Major and colleagues (2005) looked at comprehension of regional, ethnic, and international varieties of English by native and non-native speakers of English. Lectures were recorded in southern American English, African-American English, Australian English, subcontinental Indian English, and Standard American English. Both native and non-native listeners were affected by the speaker's dialect. ELLs found southern American and Standard American equally intelligible. They scored lower when listening to all the other dialects, which were all basically equivalent in terms of student test scores. The researchers offer no definitive statements on the results, though they do say that familiarity might have been a factor.

American research universities employ a large number of ELLs as teaching assistants (ITAs). Kang (2010) recommends attention to suprasegmental features in ITA training programs. Kang's research concentrated on listeners' judgments of intelligibility and accentedness, not actual comprehension. However, the paper suggests that appropriate pause placement and duration, speech rate, word stress, and varied intonation are all important considerations in improving ratings of comprehensibility and accentedness.

Pragmatic Comprehension ⸻

Pragmatic comprehension is another possible difficulty, but one that does not make the lists because it's an aspect of interactive listening, listening to another person, and studies of listening difficulties focus on students listening to lectures or audio. We will see in Myth 6 that interactive listening has been neglected in listening research.

Pragmatics is concerned with the appropriate use of language in social interactions, with topics like politeness, conversational rules, and speech acts (for example, apologizing, requesting, refusing). Though much has been written about pragmatic production, not much has been written about pragmatic comprehension.

Garcia (2004) says that learners must use pragmatic comprehension to, in her words:

- understand a speaker's intentions
- interpret a speaker's feelings and attitudes
- differentiate speech act meaning
- evaluate the intensity of a speaker's meaning, such as the difference between a suggestion and a warning
- recognize sarcasm, joking, and other facetious behavior
- be able to respond appropriately

(pp. 1–2)

What determines how good students are at pragmatic comprehension? Taguchi (2008) summarizes previous research and finds that degree of indirectness, knowledge of conventional language (chunks), cultural knowledge, linguistic proficiency, length of residence, and context of learning are all possible features in pragmatic comprehension.

Garcia's (2004) study specifically looked at comprehension of speech acts and conversational implicature (recognizing the speaker's attitude, feelings, etc.). Garcia researched the effects of proficiency (high and low) on linguistic and pragmatic comprehension. Her high group consisted of 16 TESL/Applied Linguistics graduate students whose first language was not English, and her low group consisted of 19 students in an intensive English program.

The subjects listened to dialogues of authentic service encounters between students and other students and between students and university faculty and staff. The subjects were asked both linguistic comprehension questions (concerning main ideas, details, and predictions) and pragmatic comprehension questions (concerning speech acts and implicatures). Results showed that there was a significant difference in scores for high and low groups on all measures: linguistic comprehension, pragmatic comprehension, and subsections for speech acts and implicatures. There was a relatively low overlap in linguistic scores for both groups, suggesting that linguistic listening ability (for main ideas, details, predicting/inferencing) is different from pragmatic comprehension. The high group showed greater overlap between the two abilities, suggesting that as learners become more proficient, they are able to process both types of knowledge simultaneously. The results also showed virtually no overlap in comprehension abilities for speech acts and implicatures, suggesting that a student could be good at one and not the other. Garcia concludes by calling for more classroom work on pragmatics.

You may be wondering at the comparison between low- and high-level students. Isn't it natural that higher would out-perform lower? Yes, but having two levels, in a way, allows you to see the larger issues—for example, whether linguistic and pragmatic comprehension are the same thing or different things (different, but proficiency has an effect) and if speech act comprehension is different from comprehending implicatures (probably).

Two studies by Taguchi (2005, 2008) investigated pragmatic comprehension. Taguchi (2005) compared L1 English-speaking university students and Japanese university learners of English on speed and accuracy of comprehension of conversational implicatures in English. Not surprisingly, native English speaker comprehension of English conversational implicatures was generally accurate, fast, and uniform, while learners were less accurate and slower. What was of more interest was the differences in comprehension of more and less conventional implicature. More conventional items were indirect requests and refusals. These took advantage of fixed phrases (such as *I was wondering if you could . . .*). Less conventional items were opinions and indirect information like

> John: How was the wedding? I bet it was exciting.
>
> Mary: Well . . . the cake was OK.
>
> (Taguchi, 2005, p. 549)

The more conventional items were significantly easier to comprehend and took less time to understand than the less conventional items. While overall language proficiency had a strong effect on how accurate the students were, the speed of comprehension was not predicted by how proficient a student was.

In her 2008 study, Taguchi took a similar approach to American university learners of Japanese as a foreign language. Again, proficiency had an effect on accuracy (intermediates scored higher than beginners) but not on speed. (You would expect more proficient students to be faster because their language is more automatized.) Indirect refusals (*Sorry, I have to study*) were easier to understand, and conventional indirect opinions (the question *Soo kana*—meaning *Is that so?*—to indicate reservation, but not direct disagreement) were the most difficult.

In both studies, Taguchi points out that the effect of speed on comprehension may not be visible in the populations studied, beginning and intermediate language learners. It may be that the integration of skills necessary for pragmatic comprehension is not available until advanced proficiency is reached. The foreign language element may also be significant, in that learners are not likely to get input outside the classroom and improved speed may rely on practice.

Taguchi (2008) discusses the notion of conventionality. Some issues in conventionality are frequency (do students hear it a lot and in many contexts?), degree of overlap between the ways that a given speech act is performed (indirect requests are similar in many languages), and the extent to which there is a fixed form, a chunk, that is used to do the act (in Japanese, *chotto*, which literally means *a little,* is used to signal reservations). Teachers need to have a sense of the overlap between first and target languages and teach pragmatics accordingly.

Individual Differences ——

Ultimately, listening abilities and problems are, to some extent, individual. There is a well-established sub-field of applied linguistics that concerns itself with individual differences in language acquisition and use, but very little of the research, with the exception of some on strategies, aptitude, motivation and anxiety, specifically addresses listening. Of course, listeners are more generally language learners, so they are influenced by other factors such as personality, learning/cognitive styles, creativity, self-esteem, willingness to communicate, and their beliefs about learning (Dörnyei, 2005). We have briefly discussed the role of aptitude in Myth 1. We will address strategies extensively in Myth 8. Here we will briefly look at motivation and anxiety.

Motivation, at least in terms of research, tends to be seen as a construct that applies to learning in general. However, Graham (2006) and Vandergrift (2006), in the discussion sections of their papers, raise the issue of the importance of motivation to listening. Graham (2006) says that giving more practice that students already find difficult will only demotivate. She calls for teaching students how to listen, both in top-down and bottom-up modes. Vandergrift (2006) calls for more research into motivation as a potential explanation for the remaining variance in L2 listening ability. Teachers see motivation in listening most clearly in students' outside-the-classroom listening, in their desires to watch movies or listen to music in the foreign language. To the extent that we can, and often at the expense of showing how clueless we are, we do regularly bring authentic input like songs and TV shows into the classroom (See Myth 7).

Anxiety is something else that teachers understand about listening. We understand that the very mention of listening can stress more than a few students. There have been recent attempts to see more exactly how anxiety affects listening comprehension (Elkhafaifi, 2005b; Mills, Pajares, & Herron, 2006; Berkleyen, 2009), but to my mind we are in the early stages of understanding the relationship, though we know it's there.

Listening Difficulties: A Wrap Up ⎯⎯

This chapter has focused on a few of the difficulties learners have listening. Since we're halfway through the book. I thought I would summarize some issues and introduce a few more by way of a chart breaking listening difficulty into four factors: text, task, speaker, and listener. Table 19 is based on handouts Marc Helgesen and I have provided over the years and is our understanding of ideas presented by Anderson & Lynch (1988), Buck (2001), and Nunan (2004).

TABLE 19: Why Is Listening Difficult?

The Text

- **Aspects of language:** speech rate; pausing; unfamiliar words; unfamiliar pronunciation of familiar words; unfamiliar intonation of sentences; unfamiliar grammatical structures; problems with functional language (speech acts); pragmatics
- **Amount of language:** redundancy, repetition processed as simply more language
- **Organization of text:** text not presented linearly; off-topic comments
- **Content:** familiarity of topics; number of topics in text
- **Amount of context:** co-text; roles of speakers
- **Text type:** dialogue, debate, narrative, joke, etc.

The Task

- **Complexity:** number of steps; demands on prior knowledge; proximity of necessary information; time frame
- **Level of response required:** box checking, which is easier than blank filling, which is easier than word writing, which is easier than summarizing
- **Level of participation:** possible roles are over-hearer, conversational partner, etc.
- **Knowledge of task content and procedure**
- **Level of support/context:** availability of planning time; presence of pictures
- **Response time:** time between listening and response; presence of time pressure to complete task

---

The Speaker (note many of these categories overlap with the listener in interactive speaking):

- **Style**
- **Accent**
- **Number of speakers**
- **Recorded speech or live**

The Listener

- **Proficiency level**
- **Interest and motivation**
- **Confidence/anxiety**

What We Can Do . . .

So listening is difficult. What can we do? First, I believe that if we teach learners to think about their purpose for listening, we add to the facilitating effects that other forms of pre-teaching have. Second, as a way to review the first half of the book, I review the listening process and offer specific tasks that address the various micro-skills involved.

1. Make students aware of their purposes for listening.

We can help students listen more effectively and mitigate some of their difficulties if we spend some time teaching them about the purposes for listening. We always have a purpose for listening. We may listen to the radio in the morning to decide whether to wear a coat or take an umbrella. We may listen to a song for pleasure. We listen in different ways based on our purpose. Having a purpose helps us listen more effectively. For example, when listening to a weather report, if our purpose is to decide whether to take an umbrella, we listen for the word *rain* and maybe a percentage. If we want to know whether to wear a coat, we want to focus on the temperature. In English, we listen with extra care to the end of the phrase that begins with *highs in the*—which is routinely used to indicate the warmest temperature that we can expect for the day.

There are many ways to listen, but this section presents a possible pedagogical model to introduce the idea of flexible listening. Systematically presenting listening for main ideas; listening for details; and listening and making inferences helps students develop a sense of why they listen and which skill to use to listen better (see Song, 2008, for some support for three kinds of listening). Teachers can help students be better independent listeners by asking them to focus on their reason for listening.

One way to do that is to use a simple dialogue like this one in order to show how they might listen differently depending on their goals.

> *Woman:* We're going out to dinner after class. Do you want to come, too?
>
> *Man:* Maybe. Where are you going?
>
> *Woman:* Pizza King.
>
> *Man:* Pizza? I love pizza!
>
> (Brown and Smith, 2007, p. 4)

The first kind of listening is listening for the main idea. You might set this sort of task: What's the most important idea in this conversation? What is the main thing they are talking about? Write some choices on the board: *Class? Dinner?* Students would answer "dinner." Point out that to be successful, they didn't need to understand anything else. They just had to understand that "dinner" is the main idea of the conversation. Listening for main ideas means that the listener wants to get a general idea of what is being said. The details are less important. Incidentally, rather than focus on the topic, you could ask which function is being expressed: inviting. That's another kind of main idea question.

There are other ways to listen. We sometimes need to listen for details. To point this out, use the same dialogue, but this time set this task: What are they going to eat? When students answer "pizza," point out that to be successful, they needed only to understand one detail of the conversation: that the woman and her friends are going out for pizza, not hamburgers or spaghetti. We need the details when we are getting directions to some place like a friend's home. Just understanding the topic in this case does us no good.

A third important reason for listening is listening and making inferences. Speakers do not always say exactly what they mean. That is, important aspects of meaning are sometimes implied rather than stated. Listeners have to "listen between the lines" to figure out what is really meant.

To get this point across, again use the pizza dialogue. This time ask, *Is the man going to go with them?* Point out that the man says that he loves pizza, so he probably will go. Sometimes people do not say exactly and directly what they mean. Students need practice in listening between the lines.

Let's add to the steps for successful pre-listening tasks that we explored previously. After prior knowledge has been activated and language forms have been dealt with, students can identify their purpose for listening and look at the instructions on the page to understand the situation (e.g., *Some friends are talking about what they did last weekend*). Knowledge of the situation helps activate prior knowledge as well, and gives students some idea of what to expect.

We can combine the ideas in the last two chapters (Myths 2 and 3) for a revised list of pre-listening tasks (see Table 20). Students can use the tasks to make a listening plan to think about how they will approach the listening task. I've said that we don't want to spend a great deal of time on pre-listening, so you might want to pick and choose the questions based on the difficulty of the listening task itself.

TABLE 20: Revised List of Things to Do before Listening

Warming Up

1. What's the topic?
2. Write five things you know about the topic.
3. Look at the word list. Check the words you know.

Before You Listen

1. What's your purpose for listening? Circle it.

   main idea   listening for details   inference

2. Look at instructions. What's the situation?
3. Look at the pictures. Write words.
4. Look at the choices you have.

Now make a LISTENING PLAN. Think about:

- what you know
- your answers to the questions above
- what you will FOCUS on

If students know why they are listening, they are more focused. Think back to the statement that the human mind is limited in its ability to process information. Activating prior knowledge, working on bottom-up processes through dictations and other tasks, and understanding the purpose for listening dramatically reduce the burdens on listeners.

2. Use a variety of tasks.

MICRO-SKILLS

Let's review where we've been in the first four chapters. To listen, someone needs at least the following microskills.

First, the listener needs the ability to hold language in working memory in order to make it available for processing and ultimately comprehension. Individual working memory capacity varies, and this fact may help explain a lot about individual differences in language acquisition.

The listener needs a number of sound-related skills, including:

- discrimination of individual sounds (for example, the ability to discriminate minimal pairs like *bit* and *bet*)
- recognition of the unstressed and stressed forms of words when they appear in sentences, as well as recognition of reduced forms (*wanna* for *want to*)
- knowledge of stress patterns of individual words and phrases and what stress means (the difference between "*I* went to the store" and "I went to the *store*")
- recognition of the intonation patterns of the language (statements, yes/no questions, *wh-* questions)
- ability to recognize individual words and where one word stops and another starts

Listeners also need vocabulary information. They need to:

- recognize words that are key to understanding
- ignore words they don't understand, or at least not get hung up on them
- recognize cohesive devices, the words that glue discourse together, like transition words (*so, thus, next*)

Listeners need syntactic information. They need to know the typical—and atypical—sentence patterns of a language and what shifts in meaning are signaled by the use of one or the other. They combine word and grammatical knowledge when they successfully guess the meaning of words in context and also when they recognize the function of the conversation, what the participants are trying to accomplish.

Listeners must be able to recognize, but also infer, meanings, situations, goals, participants, and participant roles. They must understand the relationship between the main idea and the details.

Listeners must listen strategically. They must understand their reasons and goals for listening and adapt them as the conversation goes on. They have to be able to signal comprehension and incomprehension. They have to know how to use their background knowledge and experience, as well as any paralinguistic information (body language, tone of voice, etc.). They have to be able to handle different rates of delivery, pauses, and self-corrections by the speaker.

While they are doing all this, they need to constantly form an overall representation of what the input is about, changing that understanding as new information is received.

All that having been said, I don't want to imply that we simply go through the list of skills and teach each one. What I would say is that we need a balance.

IDEAS FOR LISTENING TASKS

To me, that there are so many micro-skills needed for listening implies the necessity of lots of different types of listening activities. There are dozens of possible listening tasks, more than I can outline here, but here are a few.

WORD-LEVEL TASKS

- Order words.
- Count uses of a word or sound.
- Count words in a sentence.
- Identify stress in word or sentence.
- Identify intonation in sentence by drawing up/down arrows.
- Identify pauses in a script.
- Identify form of the word used (present/past).

MAIN IDEA–BASED TASKS

- Decide what the topic is.
- Given a list of possible topics, decide which one is correct.
- Paraphrase/summarize what you heard.
- Choose the correct summary statement from among several.
- Decide what is the function of the conversation. Are the speakers informing, inviting, making recommendations?
- Predict what happens next.

- Draw a picture or pictures of what happened.
- Order pictures.
- Find differences between a text and picture.

DETAIL-BASED TASKS

- List the topics that were talked about.
- From a list, check off the topics talked about.
- Add extra information to the list of topics.
- Focus on a particular category. How many males/females speaking?
- Identify a series of steps or events.
- When the teacher stops the audio, decide what is a possible next line.
- Fill in a grid, chart, or map.

INFERENCE-BASED TASKS

Obviously, these tasks are used when the answers are not directly stated in the text.

- Decide what the context is. How do you know?
- Decide who the speakers are. What is their relationship? How do you know?
- Determine what the speakers' emotions are. How strongly do they feel? How do you know?
- Given a list, sort information that is true for each speaker or was said by each speaker.

Lund's (1990) taxonomy for teaching listening is also relevant for designing tasks, as shown in Table 21.

TABLE 21: Lund's (1990) Taxonomy for Teaching L2 Listening

Listening Function (what the listener must process):
- identification (recognize words, discriminate between words or sounds)
- orientation (recognize topic, situation, participants, roles, tone, etc.)
- main idea comprehension
- detail comprehension
- full comprehension (integrating main idea and detail)
- replication (repetition, dictation, working with transcript)

Listening Response (what the learner does to demonstrate successful listening)
- doing (responding in actions, building something, etc.)
- choosing (from alternatives, ordering pictures, etc.)
- transferring (drawing a picture, filling in a map, etc.)
- answering (questions)
- condensing (making outlines, taking notes)
- extending (providing an ending)
- duplicating (taking dictation, translating, etc.)
- modeling (speaking after hearing a model)
- conversing

5

Listening means listening to conversations.

In the Real World . . .

The old language learner joke goes, "I knew my half of the dialogue, but the French guy didn't." Teachers and students seem to love dialogues. They certainly are easy to teach, and to "learn": listen, repeat, work with a partner. Then there's the real world. The French guy doesn't know the other half. But dialogues, or pieces of them, can be useful. A large amount of daily conversation is frozen speech, chunks of language, so it is good for students to learn some phrases that they can readily use while they are working on the more difficult parts of the conversation; in other words, at their best, conversations or dialogues can lead to fluency.

Historically, in general English classes, we have used dialogues (usually recorded and played for the students) to contextualize the vocabulary and grammatical structures of the unit. Students listen to the conversation, and then replicate it with the whole class and/or a partner. In most textbooks dedicated to teaching listening, the scripts are usually in dialogue form. One exception to this rule are textbooks devoted to academic lecture listening. In these books, students hear long stretches of either authentic or simulated lecturing and learn to take notes. Another exception is authentic materials that we bring into class—movies, TV shows, and songs. These are all relatively long-form, narrative-based listening.

What the Research Says . . .

In this chapter, I want to ask if we sometimes give too much emphasis to conversation in listening materials. There are many other ways we listen. The purpose of this chapter is to present research on listening to longer stretches of discourse. In fact, we have already seen many studies that have used narrative input, such as those on advance organizers and on students' difficulties listening to lectures. In those cases, the form of the input was not the issue. That is, the researchers were not looking at the role of advance organizers or the role of vocabulary on lecture comprehension versus conversation comprehension. In this chapter, we will first look at multimedia listening (input either presented on DVD or computer). The focus of much, but not all, of this research has been on multimodality, using reading skills in conjunction with listening skills, in other words on the use of captions, so I could have included it in Myth 1. However, I have two rationales for including it here: The first is that many of the caption studies concern themselves with viewing lectures or other "educational" videos, and the second that the role of captions is of interest to teachers most when they want to use movies in the classroom. Next, I will address the classic one-way listening task, dictation; newer versions of this old method incorporate narrative. Finally, I will briefly look at lecture listening, which is a specialized form of listening of great interest to many, but by no means all. Thus, I will only outline a few of its main issues. I would have liked to complete this section on research with some attention to research on stories, but it seems that, while there is some interest among English L1 acquisition researchers and discourse analysts (e.g., Brown, 1995, on the demands of listening to narratives in L1), there is little research of an empirical nature related to second language listening. I will content myself with offering the use of stories as something we can do in response to the need for extensive listening.

Video and Multimedia ——

It would be difficult to find a language program today that doesn't use either video or computers, or both, to teach listening. A relatively early comparison of audiotape, videotape, and multimedia (computer-based) listening by Brett (1997) found multimedia the most effective way to deliver a course, measured by how much the students understood of the input. He suggests that the instant feedback regarding right and wrong answers that students got while listening kept them on track and led to scores that were superior to the other groups. Hulstijn (2003) argues that an important use of multimedia in listening development is training in automatic word recognition. He presents 123LISTEN, a computer program that allows aural text to be edited into smaller segments and played with a delayed or simultaneous transcript.

The addition of visuals to sound when using video or multimedia has also been widely seen as productive to learning. We saw in Myth 2 some of the facilitative effect of visuals on comprehension. Visuals also potentially allow for viewing gestures, and the role of gestures in listening comprehension is important (Harris, 2003; Sueyoshi & Hardison, 2005). Hoven's (1999) model for listening and viewing comprehension has been influential among instructional designers. Given the frequent use of movies and television shows in classrooms, Hoven says that the idea of viewing comprehension should be added to the idea of listening comprehension. To fully understand most situations, the viewer needs to attend to the paralinguistic aspects of listening comprehension: kinesics (body language and gestures), proxemics (physical distance and touch), and prosody (stress, intonation, rhythm)—the last of which, of course, is not available visually. [See Rubin (1995) for a practical guide to using video in classrooms and Vanderplank (2010) for a research overview of language laboratories, television, and video in language teaching.]

An important part of using video and multimedia in the classroom is motivation. Students like classroom activities that look like real life.

The first question that arises when a teacher starts to use video in class is: Should I use the captions? Movies and television programs for years now have routinely come with "closed captioning," which can be turned off; captioning frequently comes in several languages. Technically, captions and soundtrack match, while subtitles and audio are in different languages, but the terminology is not always consistent in studies. There have been a number of studies on the use of captions. From Myth 2, remember Chung's (1999) study comparing the comprehension of a video with an advance organizer plus captions to one with captions only; in that case, captions were the decisive treatment.

Markham, Peter, and McCarthy (2001) investigated the use of Spanish, English, and no captions accompanying a Spanish language video about the U.S. space program. Their subjects were 169 intermediate (fourth semester) Spanish learners at a university in the United States. Students watched a seven-minute video once and were asked to write a summary and take a multiple choice test. The group that listened with L1 English subtitles performed significantly better on both measures, recall and test, than the group that listened with L2 Spanish captions. Both groups had significantly higher scores than the group that listened without any support. The results were similar in Markham and Peter (2003). The researchers suggest that in the future it would be interesting to test whether a sequence of English subtitles, Spanish captions, and nothing at all while viewing a piece of audio three times would lead to improved comprehension. Of course, for some teachers, the use of the first language should be avoided at all costs. Would students come to depend on the translation? It's an empirical question.

Taylor (2005) reviews a number of studies that show that captioning improves comprehension but claims that research on beginning students is scarce. The argument has been that it is very difficult for beginning students to read and listen in a foreign language at the same time. Taylor studied 85 beginning L1 English speakers in their second semester of Spanish. He divided the group into two smaller groups, first-year students, who had no Spanish other than the previous semester, and third-year students, who, though they were in the same class as the first-years, had prior study of three to four years (it is not explicitly stated, but these would doubtless be students who studied Spanish in high school). The students were divided into captions/no captions groups and shown a ten-minute video clip that accompanied their regular textbook. The topic was food in Latin America and Spain; both groups got a vocabulary preview. The measures were a free recall and a multiple choice test. No notes were taken. Overall, there were no significant differences between the captions and no captions groups. The third-year captions group did outperform the first-year captions groups in free recall, but there was no difference in the two no captions groups. The difference was that the first-years scored lower when given captions than with no captions. That is, captioning actually hurt the less experienced learners, while it neither helped nor hurt the more experienced. Over one-third of the first-years reported finding the captions distracting or confusing. Taylor suggests that if the first-years were given more practice using captions, they might improve because the third-years were not distracted. There is much that is mixed up here, and I think a number of factors like proficiency, time listening, and time listening with captions need to be separated out, but the idea that beginners might have difficulty doing too many things at once is not surprising.

The issue of first and second language captioning is combined with the issue of modality (audio/video) in Guichon and McLornan (2008). They remark that video provides context, but it also can be distracting. The example I always give my students is of the news. As I was writing this chapter, oil was pouring into the Gulf of Mexico. The visuals were of burning oil and oil slicks, while the announcer talked about the attendant political problems. In this case, the visual was not only *not* supporting the audio, but it was also clashing with it. Guichon and McLornan (2008) looked at four conditions: audio only, audio plus video, audio plus video plus target language (English) subtitles, and audio plus video plus L1 (French) captions. Forty intermediate L1 French learners of English watched a short BBC news report twice, took notes both times, and then wrote a summary. Both of the caption groups remembered more details than the no captions groups. The groups were too small for statistical analysis, but the English captions group remembered 30.2 percent of ideas and the French captions group 29.7 percent of ideas. The no captions group recalled 19.7 percent. By the way, if you are not terribly impressed by the percentages, in my experience this is not an uncommon outcome for the sorts of studies that divide texts into idea units and ask subjects to recall as many as they can. Guichon and McLornan (2008) did find effects for the ideas in which the audio voice-over did not match the video; these ideas were difficult to remember.

Captions typically follow along and match the visuals. Would providing the complete transcript have a greater effect than captioning? Grgurovic and Hegelheimer (2007) investigated this question with respect to software help options. Eighteen students with different home languages were divided into higher- and lower-intermediate groups. They viewed a specially constructed video that simulated a university lecture; it was eleven minutes long. The lecture was broken into short segments of 30 to 90 seconds each, and a multiple choice question was asked after each segment; there were also four post-listening questions. Students could choose to get help with the questions for which they provided incorrect answers. They had the choice of captioned video or a transcript and video. They could repeat the video as often as they liked and take as much time as they liked. If they missed a question, they answered a modified version of the question with choices in a different order. They were also provided with an online dictionary, but not one of the students used it. Though students displayed different preferences—and only 45 percent used help at all—captioning was used almost twice as much as the transcript. The authors speculate that captioning is a part of language learners' everyday experience when viewing movies, and indeed the five students who used captioning exclusively said that they routinely watched DVDs with captions. One interesting finding is that the four students who did not use any tools at all were lower-intermediate students; perhaps they were overwhelmed. In a delayed recall three weeks later, students who used captions had the best recall scores. Non-users could not recall any ideas.

Some researchers have looked at captioning's role in vocabulary acquisition. Markham (1999) tested word recognition by 118 advanced students in a university intensive program. The students had watched parts of two public television documentaries, one on whales and one on the history of civil rights. Those who viewed with captions scored higher on vocabulary tests that asked them to fill in blanks in sentences with words from the videos; in a relatively rare procedure, both sentences and alternative answers were spoken, not written. However, no gains were found for acquiring vocabulary through captioning in either the native (English) or target (Spanish) language in a study that used authentic Spanish films with American university students (Stewart & Pertusa, 2004).

Jones and Plass (2002) investigated vocabulary and the role of annotations, analogous to captions, but used in computer-assisted learning. They provided 171 students of French at an American university with a short historical text with a number of ways to understand individual words while listening to the input, either a written translation of key vocabulary, a picture of the item, both translation and picture, or no support. They studied both comprehension and vocabulary acquisition and tested both immediately and then three weeks later. For immediate recall of ideas, students who were able to see both a translation and picture while listening did marginally better than students who were provided only a picture. Those provided a picture did significantly better than the translation group. All did better than those who had no support. In the delayed test, both the picture-plus-translation and picture-only groups performed significantly better than the other groups, and the translation group had no advantage over the no support group. For vocabulary, in the immediate condition, the picture-plus-translation group outperformed all others and there was no significant difference between the picture-only and translation-only groups, though each did better than the group with no support. In the delayed test, the groups with support remembered more words than the no support group, but the only difference among the supported groups was between the picture-plus-translation group and the translation group. Thus, more support is better, and there might be some advantage to pictures over translation in the recall of ideas.

All in all, it seems that captions are reasonably effective in increasing comprehension because they give extra information. There may be proficiency effects, which is to say that beginners may be overwhelmed by too much information. None of the studies addressed the accuracy of the captions.

TABLE 22: Studies on Captions and Listening Comprehension

Effective?	**Yes:** Chung (1999), Markham, Peter, & McCarthy (2001), Markham & Peter (2003), Guichon & McLornan (2008) **No:** Taylor (2005)
Which language?	**L1>L2:** Markham, Peter & McCarthy (2001) **L1=L2:** Markham & Peter (2003), Guichon & McLornan (2008)

Dictation ——

Dictation has made something of a comeback in language learning in the past 20 years. It has changed to fit into the communicative classroom, often moving from single sentences to longer texts. Dictation, as I mentioned briefly earlier, is useful for teaching students about bottom-up processes.

Though dictation is sometimes used in studies as a form of data collection, two studies have tested dictation as a method of instruction. In a study based in an Iranian private language institute, Kiany and Shiramiry (2002) compared two groups of students, one whose listening input was from the textbook and the other whose input was the textbook as well as eleven dictations over the length of the course. The dictations came from the textbook's reading passages and conversations. The measurement was a standardized 40-item listening test for native English speakers. The dictation part of the lessons was preceded by a schema activation activity. The dictation was heard once without pauses and then again with pauses at meaningful chunks. The students then listened to check and then checked again against a transcript. Sometimes there was another listening of the whole piece. The mean gain score for the dictation group was significantly better than for the non-dictation group.

Reinders (2009) compared dictation to two other grammar-oriented tasks, one individual reconstruction of the text and the other a collaborative reconstruction. Twenty-eight upper-intermediate English learners heard a text containing negative adverbs that require subject/auxiliary verb inversion (*Never have I seen anything like this*). They heard the text three times. The two measures were correct suppliance of the target structure and a grammaticality judgment test (correct/incorrect). The dictation group heard the text once without being able to take notes. Then they heard it twice more in smaller chunks (8–10 words) and had to type it. The individual reconstructors listened, took notes, and then typed the text while thinking aloud. The collaborative condition had pairs reconstructing the text, talking it through. The uptake measure, correct use of the structure, improved with each listening for each group. Both the dictation group and the collaborative group scored significantly higher than the individual reconstruction group, but the dictation group, while better, was not significantly better than the collaborative group. There was no effect for group in the grammaticality judgment test, though all improved their scores for the sentences with negative adverbs, compared to the sentences without them that served as distractors. Though the dictation group performed better by the uptake measure, they listened in shorter spurts, so they had less stress on working memory and didn't have to rely as much on schemata as the other groups who were reconstructing the entire text at once.

Most dictation used today is dictogloss, which is based on longer texts and less emphasis on exact replication of the teacher's words than on plausible, grammatically correct answers that maintain the original meaning of the passage. Students listen to a passage read at normal speed, take notes, and use those notes to work with a partner to reconstruct the passage as well as they can. They pool their individual proficiencies to negotiate a plausible reproduction. If you haven't heard of dictogloss, more information is provided in the *What Can We Do?* section (pp. 103–106).

Dictogloss has theoretical underpinnings. Schmidt (2001) has stressed the role of attention in language learning. One aspect of attention is noticing, which Schmidt calls "the first step in language building"(p. 31). Though there is debate on the exact role and processes of attention, at some level, for learners to learn, they need to notice features in the input in order for those features to become intake and available for acquisition. One way this is done is through the noticing of the gap between what the learner knows and the target form (Thornbury, 1997). Swain and her colleagues (Swain & Lapkin, 1995; Swain, 2000) have done a number of experiments with Canadian secondary students in what Swain has called "pushed output." Pushed output means that students are given the opportunity to work with their own spoken (taped interactions) or written (compositions) output, individually or in pairs, to realize what they don't know, to form hypotheses about what might be correct, and to test those hypotheses. Swain and Lapkin (1995) call the talk about language that occurs "language-related episodes," and they show how students are able to discuss and resolve the gaps in their knowledge together through a "collaborative dialogue" (Swain, 2000). Dictogloss combines listening, writing, and discussions that potentially lead to language-related episodes and collaborative dialogue, and thus promotes noticing.

Dictogloss also encourages learner autonomy, cooperative learning, and critical thinking. It supports content-based instruction and can serve as an alternative assessment (Jacobs & Small, 2003).

Two studies have looked at the interactional aspect of the reconstruction stage of dictogloss. Does the pair work make a difference in acquiring language forms, or would an individual reconstruction be just as effective? Kuiken and Vedder (2002) found that interaction made no difference in acquisition of the passive voice (*Hamlet was written by Shakespeare.*), though their qualitative analysis of the data did show that interaction led to noticing the passive form. Kim (2008) found that Korean as a second language learners who performed the dictogloss reconstruction collaboratively learned more vocabulary.

Dictogloss was compared to a jigsaw task in Swain and Lapkin (2001). The jigsaw task was for pairs of students to write a story based on eight pictures. Each student had half the pictures, odd and even numbers in the sequence. The students told each other their half of the stories; then they wrote the complete story together. The dictogloss was based on a combination of the individual telling of the story in the pictures by three native speakers of French.

First of all, the dictogloss pairs behaved more like each other in terms of how long they took to complete the task, the number of times they discussed a particular language point, and scores on vocabulary use. This makes sense because a dictogloss is more of a closed task than a jigsaw, which allows for more differentiation in completion.

Dictogloss students also performed better in using the target grammatical structures when telling the story, though there was no significant difference on the average between the groups on the grammar and vocabulary tests that were administered. The dictogloss students attempted more complex vocabulary and syntactic structures, perhaps because they were dealing with a sophisticated text instead of pictures. Dictogloss students, for probably the same reason, wrote in paragraphs rather than simply numbering descriptions of the pictures, which many of the jigsaw students did. Both groups focused equally on form, perhaps because there was a grammar-focused lesson beforehand, or perhaps because both groups were writing, which might be perceived as an accuracy activity.

Two studies have compared the efficacy of dictogloss to that of Processing Instruction. Processing Instruction (PI) is identified with VanPatten and his colleagues. PI focuses on changing learners' processing strategies in ways that help them understand input more effectively, making it available ultimately for acquisition. It works on the input and constrains, or influences, how it is processed. For example, English learners of Spanish bring a "noun first" strategy to understanding Spanish sentences. While in English the subject usually precedes the verb, in Spanish the subject is frequently dropped or the object can occur before the subject. Thus, English learners of Spanish often misunderstand who likes or sees whom, for example. PI-based programs

go through a series of tasks to force students out of such inefficient processing strategies (misunderstandings). All work is comprehension
based, and students do not actually produce the target structures
(VanPatten, 1996).

Qin (2008) compared PI with a modified form of dictogloss in
which her beginning Chinese learners of English read the input, which
was designed to teach the passive voice. Qin found in the immediate
post-test that PI outperformed dictogloss in comprehension measures
and dictogloss performed as well as PI in production measures. One
month later, both groups performed similarly, so any advantage had
been lost; both groups improved from the pre-test, however. Qin pronounced both dictogloss and PI as potentially useful pedagogically.

VanPatten and his colleagues (VanPatten, Inclezan, Salazar, &
Farley, 2009) criticized Qin's learning tasks and assessment methods.
They studied the learning of direct object pronouns and word order in
Spanish by U.S. university students, comparing dictogloss with PI and
a control group. They reported the results on three measures: an interpretive task (matching pictures to sentences), a sentence-level production task (filling in blanks), and a reconstruction task (like a dictogloss
reconstruction, but individually done). The interpretive task saw all
groups making gains, but with the advantage to PI, which also held its
gains in the post-test. There was a slight advantage for PI over the control group in the sentence task, but overall no significant differences. PI
did perform better than the others on the delayed post-test. The reconstruction task was seen as perhaps too difficult, as there were no significant gains and no advantage for PI. Thus, VanPatten et al. claim
superiority for PI over dictogloss.

Finally, there is a related study by Lynch (2001) on student transcription that is relevant to this section. Lynch describes a procedure
and a pilot study that grew out of what he calls "proof-listening." In
this procedure, an interactive pair task is recorded and played three
times in front of the class. First, the original pair comments and corrects, then the other members of the class join in, and, finally, the
teacher comments. For Lynch, the next step was for students to transcribe their task, a kind of self-dictation. He asked volunteers to tran-

scribe verbatim only two minutes of their task, producing one version of the transcript. Then they were to correct the transcript, producing a second version. He, as teacher, then intervened and reformulated the transcript for a third version. Lynch found that the students were able to re-negotiate their understanding of the task and themselves while transcribing. They were cooperative and very thorough, taking more than 45 minutes to transcribe the two minutes. On average, the four pairs found 28 things to change in the segment, and most were changed for the better. Grammatical changes greatly outnumbered lexical changes. Still, there was plenty of work for the teacher, as students corrected only 60 percent, leaving 40 percent for Lynch.

TABLE 23: Studies on the Effectiveness of Dictation and Dictogloss

Lynch (2001): students can transcribe and spot many of their own errors
Kiany & Shiraminy (2002): dictation improved listening comprehension scores
Kuiken & Vedder (2002): interaction during reconstruction phase helped students notice grammatical form
Qin (2008): both dictogloss and Processing Instruction useful
Kim (2008): students reconstructing collaboratively learned more vocabulary than those who performed the task individually
Reinders (2009): dictation improved production of one grammatical structure

Organizing Discourse: The Example of Lecture Listening ——

One issue that comes up when the discussion turns to longer texts is the ways in which the discourse is organized. Within listening research, the subfield of academic listening has been especially interested in discourse markers. Discourse markers are not the only things that make listening to lectures challenging. As we have seen elsewhere in this book, rate of speech, vocabulary, background knowledge, and use of visuals are all potential factors in comprehension. Overall, Richards (1983) lists 18 micro-skills implicated in listening to academic lectures. It would be difficult to say which factor is most important. (See Chaudron, 1995, and Flowerdew, 1994, for overviews of academic listening.)

Listening to lectures is a demanding cognitive task. Understanding the content requires that students form an overall sense of the purpose of the lecture, the likely rhetorical form it's going to take (comparison/contrast, problem/solution), and recognize many main ideas and even more supporting details. The student also has to learn to edit out the asides and digressions that most lecturers include. To help them understand, students need to be aware of and make use of the techniques that lecturers use to organize their talks. Macro-markers like *Today I want to . . .* , *There are three things . . .* serve to provide a general structure to the lecture. They are useful for separating main ideas from details and for getting a constantly updated representation of the topic. Micro-markers like *OK, well, so* operate at a more local level but are also important to understanding.

Chaudron and Richards (1986) looked at both macro- and micro-markers and their effect on lecture comprehension. They condensed a real lecture to seven pages of text and recorded the text. Subjects performed a clozed (fill in the blanks) recall of parts of the lecture at 90-second intervals and took two tests on the content of the lecture. Chaudron and Richards tested two groups of students, pre-university and academically admitted, divided into groups that heard the lecture enhanced with micro-markers, macro-markers, or both. Overall, macro-markers were more effective than micro-markers in facilitating comprehension.

Partially as a result of the early research on the efficacy of macro-markers, English for Academic Purposes (EAP) listening textbooks that prepare learners to succeed in English-medium universities have tended to focus on macro-markers at the expense of micro-markers, and perhaps for a good reason. Clerehan (1995) analyzed lecture notes from both English L1 and L2 learners in a law class in an Australian university. The L1 students recorded 99–100 percent of the main ideas in the lecture while the L2 students missed 19 percent of the main ideas and 34 percent of the ideas in the next level of idea organization, the subheadings. Clerehan suggests that they did not recognize the rhetorical structure of the lecture. If this were indeed the case, educating them as to the possible discourse markers that signpost lectures might be effective, as would teaching some common ways that speakers organize lectures. The subjects in Tauroza and Allison's (1994) study of an electrical engineering lecture at an English-medium Hong Kong university also had difficulty with rhetorical structure, in this case difficulty understanding a lecture with a more complex structure than they were used to.

The point here is that theoretically a student could understand all the individual words and still find it difficult to make sense of a lecture if the internal structure of that lecture were unclear. Another way to say this is discourse markers help activate formal or textual schemata. However, as Olsen and Huckin (1990) show, even if the lecturer makes good use of discourse markers, if the students do not understand the rhetorical structure of what they call "the point-driven lecture," they will fail to comprehend the main ideas. Nine of their 14 subjects went looking for details, and understood most of them, but missed the three main ideas that the instructor reported were the core of the lecture.

Jung (2003a, 2003b, 2006) has laid out the importance of discourse markers in comprehension generally. Her first paper (2003a) is a pilot study with only 16 students, all Korean speakers studying English in the United States. Two groups heard an audiotaped lecture on psychology and wrote summaries of the lecture. One group heard the original lecture, and the other heard the lecture with all its discourse markers removed. Those who heard the original remembered almost twice as many main ideas as the no-markers group; they also remembered more details, but not significantly more. The next study (2003b) increased the number of students to 80. These were Korean students studying in their home country. Again, those who heard the original lecture with discourse markers retained more information. Jung's final study (2006) is a qualitative look at the 2003b material showing the difficulties the students had, including missing cause-effect relationships, misunderstanding sequential information, and confusing the relationship of main ideas when topics shifted—all things that discourse markers provide the listener.

Dunkel and Davis (1994) saw no effects for discourse markers for either L1 English speakers or ELLs. Subjects listened to a lecture on the sinkings of the *Titanic* and the *Andrea Doria* and took notes, which they used to recall the lecture in L1. Though the native speakers recalled twice as many ideas as the English learners, the absence of discourse markers made no difference to the recall of either group.

The studies of Dunkel and Davis and Chaudron and Richards were critiqued in terms of research design by Flowerdew and Tauroza (1995), who chose to focus on micro-markers in their study. The most common of these were *so, right, well, and, OK, now, then, all right, because,* and *fine.* According to Flowerdew and Tauroza, these words are often found at the shift from one topic to another or from one function, like listing, to another, like offering an analogy. They signpost shifts within discourse when the topic is not congruent with the previous topic. Electrical engineering students were divided into two groups, one watching a videotaped lecture with discourse markers and the other without discourse markers. The group that viewed the original lecture with markers remembered significantly more ideas in their written summaries and on a short answer test than did the group that did not hear the discourse markers. Thus, Flowerdew and Tauroza's findings support Jung's, but focus on micro-markers. They contradict the work of Dunkel and Davis because discourse markers were found facilitative of comprehension, and Chaudron and Richards because micro-markers were effective. Morell (2004) suggests that while macro-markers are characteristic of interactive lectures, compared to non-interactive lectures, use of micro-markers is idiosyncratic among lecturers.

Two studies have been done comparing real world lectures with those in EAP listening textbooks. Flowerdew and Miller (1997) compared one lecture with five textbooks. The textbooks made regular heavy use of markers, while the lecturer was inconsistent, starting off using them and then using them irregularly. For example, Flowerdew and Miller note a case in which the lecturer signals there will be three aspects and then enumerates the first and third, but not the second. Thompson (2003) compares six real lectures to ten textbook lectures from five books. Lessons in the books were more clearly signaled than in real lectures. Books focus on topical organization and describe structure more, while real lectures use the most markers to organize the subtopics at lower levels of organization. Textbooks also tend to break up the lecture audio into shorter "phonological paragraphs" than real lecturers use. This is the use of intonation to convey topic opening and closing. Shorter paragraphs may lead to more understanding but may not prepare students for the classroom.

TABLE 24: Studies on Lecture Comprehension

Discourse markers facilitate comprehension
Yes: Jung (2003a, 2003b, 2006)
No: Dunkel & Davis (1994)
Yes, macro-markers: Chaudron & Richards (1986)
Yes, micro-markers: Flowerdew & Tauroza (1995)
Students have problems understanding the rhetorical structure of lectures
Olsen & Huckin (1990)
Clevehan (1995)
Tauroza & Allison (1994)
EAP lecture-training materials do not reflect the real world
Flowerdew & Miller (1997)
Thompson (2003)

This chapter has looked at the kinds of listening activities that go beyond short exchanges. Lecture listening is not for every group, but caption-supported video, dictation, and dictogloss offer interesting opportunities for learning.

What We Can Do . . .

1. Go beyond conversations and provide opportunities to listen to extended prose.

Two relatively easy ways to introduce language beyond conversations are dictation of longer texts and listening to stories.

DICTATION

Within the area of dictation, there are three broad areas. The first is sentence dictation, the second is communicative dictation, and the third is dictogloss (though it too is communicative).

We've probably all done sentence dictation. It's really simple: the teacher reads some sentences, usually relatively slowly, and the students write what they hear. There's nothing wrong with that, especially when you're working with English, which has complex sound-symbol correspondences (which is to say spelling rules are complicated). Dictation is also great for working with bottom-up processing.

We've gotten beyond simple sentence dictation to what we might call communicative dictation. See Table 25 on page 102 for Davis and Rinvolucri's ten good reasons for dictation, then see their (1988) book for lots of ideas for using dictation in the classroom.

TABLE 25: Rethinking Dictation

> **Ten Good Reasons to Use Dictation (Davis & Rinvolucri 1988, pp. 4–8; reasons verbatim, examples theirs, but paraphrased)**
> 1. The students are active during the exercise.
> 2. The students are active after the exercise (they can easily self-correct).
> 3. Dictation leads to oral communication activities (e.g., questions for a pair work activity can be dictated rather than simply handed out).
> 4. Dictation fosters unconscious thinking (e.g., in a task in which students are writing words to use in a story, they are really already working on the story).
> 5. Dictation copes with mixed ability groups (e.g., complete dictation for more advanced students and fill-in-the-blanks for less advanced).
> 6. Dictation deals with large groups.
> 7. Dictation will often calm groups.
> 8. Dictation is safe for the non-native teacher (the language is known).
> 9. For English, it is a technically useful exercise (because of the poor sound-symbol correspondence of English; it would be less useful for Spanish, in which one sound matches one letter).
> 10. Dictation gives access to interesting text.

"Communicative dictation" is a catch-all name for dictation that goes beyond simple transcription. Here are some ideas.

- Find the differences between spoken and written texts. The teacher (or a partner) reads one version, while the listener looks at a text that differs slightly. The listener corrects the "mistakes."
- Jigsaw listening is a procedure in which students hear different parts of a text on audio files and work to combine them. Students can also listen to two versions of the same text and work to find the differences, or work to construct a logical version of events.
- Students write dictated sentences, but add their own content at cued points.

- Teachers hold up a picture and say a mix of true and false sentences about it. Students write what is true, and change the false statement to true.
- Teachers read a sentence (e.g., about trivia) and students write whether they believe it is true or false, either separating true and false into columns or writing *I think* or *I don't think* first.

Dictogloss (Wajnryb, 1990) is a modified dictation activity in which students first listen individually and then work in groups to reconstruct the text (see Table 26 on page 104). The point of the activity is not complete accuracy, but rather students' use of their own grammatical and semantic resources. The teacher can then work with what students have, rather than deliver a canned grammar lesson. As Wajnryb (1990, p. 7) says, dictogloss "aims to upgrade and refine the learners' use of the language through a comprehensive analysis of the language options in the correction of the learners' approximate texts."

Wilson (2003) would extend the basic dictogloss procedure to a "discovering" phase. In it, students would compare their texts with the original and attempt to classify their mistakes based on categories such as *couldn't hear the sound, couldn't separate the sounds, couldn't remember the meaning of a word,* and *new word*. They would then assess the importance of their errors.

TABLE 26: Dictogloss

The Dictogloss Procedure (Wajnryb, 1990)

1. Read the text twice at normal speed.
2. Students write what words and phrases they can.
3. In groups, students pool their words and reconstruct the text to the best of their abilities. The reconstruction won't be 100% correct.
4. Class discusses and compares answers.

Discovery Listening (Wilson, 2003)

Add these steps:

5. Compare text with original text. Attempt to classify errors.
6. Assess importance of errors.
7. Listen again without text and perform self-assessment of task.

Alternatives (from eight suggested by Jacobs & Small, 2003):

1. Don't allow notes. Students just write a summary.
2. Give scrambled sentences: Text is presented sentence by sentence. Students first re-create and then re-order in logical fashion.
3. Do student-to-student dictogloss

STORIES

Using stories in the classroom is first and foremost fun. Folktales especially offer opportunities to share cultures. Here are some uses of stories; some are adapted from Morgan and Rinvolucri (1983).

- Teacher tells a story and dictates comprehension questions. Students answer the questions individually and take turns re-telling each other the story. They also have to negotiate any differences.
- After a story is told, teacher puts up a series of pictures in random order. Pairs work together to reconstruct the story.
- Students rank a teacher's list of words in order of their importance to a story they have heard.
- Students match a list of adjectives to characters in the story, or assign characters zodiac signs.

- Listen to a song. Tell the protagonist's story. Extend the story back and forward in time.
- Pairs incorporate a set of vocabulary words into a story for review, or randomly choose five words from a dictionary and make up a story using them.
- Teacher tells half the story, and students ask questions to determine the ending.
- Teacher tells a story but stops throughout to ask questions. Students fill in details through their answers to the questions.
- Students write ten words they feel are important to the story and share with a group.
- After listening, students reconstruct story in pairs from individual sentences on slips of paper (strip story).

2. Encourage narrow, extensive, and extended listening.

Students have a lot of opportunities to listen to narrative outside the classroom. The problem with listening outside the classroom is that the students are relatively unsupported. They may be able to hear the news in their own language first, building schema, and then listen in L2, but it is probably the case that much of what they can find has no equivalent. However, they can build up schema and vocabulary by listening narrowly (Krashen, 1996; Dupuy, 1999). Narrow listening means listening to the same kinds of stories, the same topics over time. Gradually, it is possible to build up expertise in a small area because the words, and sometimes even the grammatical structures, are repeated. Students get familiar with the topics through repetition, too. Ideally, students would listen to something they are passionate about.

Narrow listening is related to the idea of extensive listening. The difference is that extensive listening does not imply specialization, while narrow listening does. Extensive listening is an outgrowth of extensive reading, the idea that in order to learn to read students should read a lot and not worry about exercises and comprehension questions (Day and Bamford, 1998). Extensive listening emphasizes listening to easily understandable material in order to build listening fluency.

Rob Waring's website (robwaring.org//el) is the place to start investigating extensive listening. Waring (2010) recommends that learners use material of which they understand 90 percent of the content and 95 percent of the vocabulary, without stopping the audio—and which they enjoy. This may be audio that supplements graded readers or websites dedicated to English language learners. His site has an extensive list of recommended material.

Extended listening is the label Ur (1984) gave to listening to longer pieces of discourse and coming to some sort of conclusion about them. She included problem solving tasks, in which students might listen to something from an advice column and respond, or to a short mystery that they solve. Jigsaw listening is a technique in which different partners hear different pieces of information and either combine them to get the whole picture, or use them as input for discussion and problem solving. Ur also recommends giving students a chance to make an emotional or intellectual response to interviews, comedy, drama, advertisements, and poetry. In this case, student reaction displays comprehension. It isn't necessary to quiz them on details.

Movies and the Internet are obvious places for narrow, extensive and extended listening. I will have more to say about authentic sources in Myth 7.

MYTH **6**

Listening is an individual, inside-the-head process.

In the Real World . . .

Much of listening research has been psycholinguistic in nature. It has focused on what goes on inside the heads of individual listeners. Of course, it is very difficult to get at what people are "really" doing, so we as teachers are ultimately making inferences based on observed behavior. Because a certain percentage of the class gets an answer correct, we assume they understood. We don't know how they got to the answer or if what they did will transfer to the real world. We can, and should, ask students to reflect on their process, but I know it's sometimes difficult to do. We do see listening comprehension at work when we walk around during pair and group work activities, as speakers and listeners exchange information or opinions and negotiate language, like this:

Learner 1: John arrive, arrove—arrove or arrive?

Learner 2: arrove is in past

Learner 1: arrove airport. Or arrived?

Learner 2: arrove is in past

Learner 1: I mean arrove or arrived

(Adams, 2007, p. 48)

Oops. Or, ideally more like this:

Mai:　[. . .] Music make me ah make people . . .

Chie:　(writing) Makes

Mai:　Makes

Chie:　People

Mai:　Happy . . . comma . . . relaxing, relaxed? Relaxing?
　　　Which one? . . . Relaxed?

Chie:　Relaxed, relaxed . . . and exciting.

Mai:　Excited?

Chie:　Excited.

(Watanabe, 2008, p. 619)

Listening materials usually drive students even farther into their own heads. They usually ask learners to engage as individuals while listening. There may be a pre-listening class discussion of the topic and a post-listening whole-class checking of answers, but the "real" listening is seen as what goes on in the learner's head. I do think we can profitably have students working together to do the tasks and talk about their answers and how they got them, but some teachers have told me that they think that lets weaker students off the hook.

Despite the fact that the communicative approach to language teaching and learning, now about 40 years old, was predicated on theories about the social use of language, it's only been relatively recently that people have begun to speak of a "social turn" in language acquisition research (Block, 2003). This chapter looks at what happens when we consider listening, speaking, and social interaction all together. We will first look generally at two explanations for what goes on when students work together, the cognitive and sociocultural approaches to interaction. Then, we will drill down into each approach and present some recent studies as well as some earlier studies that seem to me to present important ideas for classroom interaction. Next, we will look specifically at the strategies that learners use when interacting in the classroom. After that, we will view larger social factors, those beyond the classroom. Finally, in preparation for the What We Can Do section, we will look at what I will facetiously call "the ideal listening task."

What the Research Says . . .

As I said in Myth 1, there are two kinds of listening, reciprocal and non-reciprocal. The research presented so far in this book, indeed most of the research done on L2 listening, concerns itself with non-reciprocal listening. Subjects listen to audio and perform tasks or try to recall what they've heard. Reciprocal listening has been ignored, relatively speaking (Vandergrift, 1997b). We in fact have lots of evidence of people listening to other people in the form of research in speaking. Studies on the role of the negotiation of meaning and the efficacy of task-based language learning have presented as evidence dialogues between pairs of students, but the unit of analysis has not been, for the most part, measurement of listening comprehension.

During a conversation, listeners are very active. They have to be on the look out for topic changes and they have to signal when they want to speak or change the topic. They have to participate in turn-taking, giving appropriate responses, including minimal, back-channel responses to encourage the listener to continue or to show understanding (e.g., *Uh huh*). Listeners have to figure out what to do when speakers' goals or claims conflict with theirs (often a question of power relationships). They have to constantly check their understanding and ask questions if they believe they're getting lost (Rost, 1990).

Erickson (1986) sums up the roles of speaker and listener this way:

Thus to talk is also to listen—to attend, by watching and hearing, to what the audience is doing from moment to moment. The speaker is not simply an information sender but is also an information receiver. Conversely, the listener is a sender as well as a receiver. (p. 315)

Erickson is adopting the "conduit metaphor" of communication here: One sends and the other receives. He is modifying that metaphor to emphasize that roles are not so clearly defined. Perhaps we should come at this in another way, a way that focuses on how meaning is co-constructed and exists in a sociocultural context.

Cognitive and Sociocultural Approaches: A General Introduction ——

Language acquisition research can be very broadly divided into cognitive and sociocultural camps, though each approach is itself divided into further groups.

As we will see, the single idea from second language research that has been most used (and sometimes abused) in L2 classrooms is the notion of the negotiation of meaning. The "negotiation of meaning" refers to the process by which those who are speaking to each other come to a common understanding of what is being communicated, as we saw in the Real World section. Negotiating meaning is a central cognitive idea, an aspect of Long's Interaction Hypothesis (Long, 1996), which says that interaction facilitates language acquisition because the conversational and linguistic adjustments that speakers make in the face of non-comprehension on the part of listeners provide the sort of input that the listeners need. The Interaction Hypothesis provided the rationale for the use of pair and group work in classrooms, and the usefulness of such work has been affirmed over and over again through the years, as we will see.

When misunderstanding occurs, whether it is a result of sounds, words, grammar, or discourse processes, listeners have numerous options for improving their comprehension. Table 27 summarizes the options. (Of course, the listener can always feign understanding and hope for the best.)

TABLE 27: Meaning-Negotiation Mechanisms

- Asking for repetition (*Pardon? What?*)
- Asking for clarification (*What does X mean? The what?*)
- Expressing non-understanding (Frowns, gestures, *I don't know X.*)
- Asking for confirmation (*You said . . . ? You mean . . . ?*)
- Interpretive summary (*So you . . .* —a paraphrase of what the speaker has said)
- Guessing (like a confirmation request, but less certain: *Is it an X?*)
- Other-repair (correcting something the speaker said—*Oh, you mean the X.*)

Adapted from Dörnyei & Kormos, 1998.

The cognitive perspective historically focused on language acquisition through constructs like modified input (see Myth 4). More recently, this perspective has been tied closely to task-based language learning. Additionally, the idea of recasts (learner or teacher reformulations of language) has supplemented the negotiation of meaning as a central idea (Skehan, 2003).

The sociocultural approach to language acquisition, following Vygotsky (1978) sees cognitive functions arising as a result of social processes. That is, dialogue is a central force in learning. Collaborative dialogue, according to Swain (2000, p. 113), "is problem-solving, and, hence, knowledge-building dialogue." Swain continues, "As each participant speaks, their 'saying' becomes 'what they said,' providing an object for reflection." Swain and her colleagues (e.g., Swain & Lapkin, 1995) provide opportunities for their students to collaboratively ponder "what they said" through the use of video or audio or through collaborative writing exercises.

Both approaches—cognitive and sociocultural—provide unique, sometimes isolated, vantage points on acquisition. We need more studies like Foster and Ohta (2005) and Nakahama, Tyler, and van Lier (2001), which look at the same data from both cognitive and sociocultural perspectives. We could use studies like theirs to generate hypotheses for a social understanding of listening within speaking tasks. Most research in conversation, which is, after all, when we probably use listening most, has ignored the listening side of the equation. What we know about listening in conversation sometimes gets lost in the products of clarification, comprehension checks, collaboration, and so on.

Recent work on conversation analysis (CA) in language development might be extended to focus on the listening side of the equation, though perhaps those in CA would not be interested in doing so. The CA work has tended to get lumped together with work in the Vygotskian paradigm, sometimes by researchers themselves. Both of these approaches are very broadly social but have different methods. Having said that, I, too will lump them together. For debate on the usefulness of sociocultural and conversation analysis approaches, see the 2007 focus issue of *Modern Language Journal* (Magnan, 2007).

Interaction in the Classroom: Selected Cognitive Studies ——

Long's Interaction Hypothesis grew out of a challenge to Krashen (1982), who claims that comprehensible input is sufficient for language acquisition. Long maintains that input is necessary but not sufficient for SLA. The cognitive interactionist studies are firmly rooted in the desire to test whether negotiation leads to acquisition, and whether some sort of input can also lead to acquisition. These studies were also connected, at least in the beginning, with those that we saw in Myth 4 that concern themselves with the relative merits of simplification and elaboration.

The classic study of the relationship of interaction and comprehension is Pica, Young, and Doughty (1987), which tested the roles of premodified input and interactionally modified input. We have see that modified input, be it simplified or elaborated, can help comprehension. In this study, an L1 speaker of English gave instructions to English language learners; the learners were to choose an item and place it in a scene. (Incidentally, native speaker/non-native speaker interaction was the norm at the beginning of this research paradigm; it was only later that researchers began to widely study non-native/non-native interaction.) A baseline version of the directions was produced by transcribing an interaction between two native English speakers. Then, a linguistically modified version was made that built in redundancy and reduced the complexity of the language. Eight subjects heard this modified input. Each direction was read once, and there was no opportunity to interact. Eight students were in the interaction condition, in which they heard the "harder" script, but could ask questions to clarify understanding. The interaction actually increased the complexity of the language, even over the baseline, but interaction also brought about significantly higher comprehension scores, a difference in the success rate of choosing and placing the objects correctly of 19 percent over the modified input condition. Interactions that had the greatest effect were characterized by frequent use of confirmation checks (*Next to the duck?*) and clarification requests (*What does X mean?*), which in turn led to repetition of the most important nouns.

Pica, Young, and Doughty (1987) was among the first in a long line of studies on the effects of interaction. (For a review, see Gass, 1997, and for a collection of articles, see Mackey, 2007.) I want to highlight a few studies in this tradition. A comprehensive overview would necessitate another book.

Loschky (1994) is a study of the acquisition of Japanese as a foreign language by university students, mostly L1 English speakers. The targets for acquisition were 34 concrete nouns and the grammar of locative sentences (*The station is this side of the park*). Listeners had to identify which object was being described in spoken sentences. There were three conditions. In the baseline condition, sentences were read once at normal speed. In the pre-modified input condition, redundant or clarifying sentences were added to the baseline sentences, and the reader was allowed to slow down the speech rate. In the interaction condition, negotiation of meaning was allowed.

Interaction led to more comprehension than the baseline or pre-modified conditions. Furthermore, those who comprehended more did not acquire more of the target words or structure. Loschky (1994) concludes that negotiation improves moment-by-moment comprehension and was especially effective on the most difficult task, but there is no necessary relationship between levels of comprehension and subsequent acquisition. What is understood does not necessarily become intake available for acquisition.

The differences between comprehension and production are highlighted in Gass and Varonis (1994). The study took place in two steps. In the first step, non-native speakers of English, students at a university intensive English program, listened to a script read by native speakers of English and placed items on a board depicting a beach scene. Overall, they comprehended better when they received modified input than they did when they received unmodified input. They did better when they were allowed to negotiate, compared to not being able to negotiate. The best combination was receiving modified input and interacting.

In the second step, the students were speakers and the native English speakers the listeners. Overall, there was no effect for interaction, but the experience of the first task seemed to influence the second. Those students who were able to interact in the first task were more successful at making themselves understood in the second. However, the students who received modified input in Task 1, and were successful at understanding, were not successful at giving directions in Task 2. It seems to me that the students who interacted the first time gained insight into the task demands more readily by doing the task.

Teachers are interested in how to implement negotiation. Many EFL classrooms are traditionally teacher-led, partially because of tradition and partially, say teachers, because large class sizes make pair work a problem. Ellis, Tanaka, and Yamazaki (1994) affirmed that interaction led to better comprehension than pre-modified input, but an interesting aspect of their research is the finding that learners who actively negotiated comprehended no better than those who simply overheard the negotiation of others. This would seem to give hope to those teachers who want to do whole-class information gap activities.

He and Ellis (1999) suggest, however, in a direct comparison of teacher-fronted and pair activities, that pair work might hold interest for students. They compared pre-modified input, interaction, and negotiated output. The task was to place furniture in an apartment. A completed picture had to reproduced by writing the number of the item in the appropriate place. In the pre-modified input condition, the teacher slowly read a set of instructions that included the definitions of each item as well as its location. In the interaction condition, the teacher read instructions minus the definitions (*Here is a cushion. Would you please put the cushion on the sofa?*) and students could negotiate the meaning of the word (*What's a cushion?*) as well as the placement of the item (p. 121). The output condition was an activity in which students wrote their own directions; they could also negotiate.

The output group was most accurate in understanding the directions, scoring significantly higher than the other two groups, which had no significant difference between their scores. That is, comprehension was best in the condition in which students negotiated meaning together. The output group was also best in remembering the words for the items and best on a test that required producing the words. He and Ellis (1999) adopt a sociocultural explanation for the results of this classic cognitive task. They see the output pairs as scaffolding each other to produce an optimal learning experience. Whereas the two teacher-fronted tasks turned out, in the opinion of He and Ellis, to be somewhat mechanical, the pair work was a joint problem-solving opportunity. Their work provides a good segue to the sociocultural approaches to interaction.

Interaction in the Classroom: Selected Sociocultural Studies ——

Listening comprehension is specifically addressed from the sociocultural point of view in Garcia and Ascención (2001). They address two questions: Does interaction have a positive effect on language development? And, if so, what features account for that development? Subjects were 39 students in beginning Spanish classes. Students in the experimental group were allowed to interact in small groups while students in the control group worked individually. Students listened to a very short (150-word) lecture on three people's daily routines and schedules. Before listening, they were given three hours of instruction on the target grammar that would be useful in comprehending the passage. After listening to the lecture, the experimental group shared their notes; the control group studied their own notes on the lecture. Everyone then reconstructed the text of the lecture from their notes, and then took a listening comprehension test, again using notes. The reconstruction was scored on grammatical accuracy of the target forms. The two groups scored similarly on the text reconstruction, but the experimental interaction group did significantly better on the listening comprehension test.

What made the interaction effective? A look at the interactions themselves found features similar to previous research. For example, students used English to question each other about Spanish usage (*What does X mean? I think it's X.*) They translated and they code-switched between Spanish and English in the middle of sentences. Finally, however, different groups took advantage of collaboration differently. Two groups, A and D, were more concerned with the content of the task and used very little Spanish. Another, C, made extensive use of Spanish. Group B asked a lot of clarification questions. Group E used a mix of questioning usage, repairing each other's errors, and confirmation questions. The last three groups, those that actively collaborated, had the highest listening test mean scores.

Much current work in the sociocultural paradigm concerns itself with a critique of the assumptions of the standard understandings and measurements of interaction. Foster and Ohta (2005) show, for example, through transcripts, cases in which the negotiation of meaning that is the focus of cognitive accounts of tasks is absent and yet, despite that, learners are still engaged in co-construction of meaning, other-correction, self-correction, use of continuers (signals that the listener is interested), and so on. Negotiation is one process among many. Learners also actively help each other and correct their own mistakes, even when there is no overt communicative breakdown.

From a conversation analysis viewpoint, Jenks (2009) argues that certain roles are inherent in information gap activities. It's important to note that Jenks is speaking of one-way tasks, in which, for example, the speaker/director has a map that the listener/navigator must follow or replicate. Of (task) necessity, the person without the missing information has to ask a series of clarification questions. The burden of comprehension is on the listener. Jenks argues that this potentially frustrates the speaker and leads to "a loss in fluidity" such that "the interaction becomes stilted and minimal" (p. 190).

Of course, the point of information gaps is to draw attention to what learners do not know in hopes of developing their language. From a pedagogical perspective, one-way tasks are generally regarded as inferior to two-way tasks in focusing attention, though they are arguably "cleaner" for research. So, teachers should use more two-way tasks. I think the prescription also is to pay attention to classroom dynamics. The sort of interactional problems that Jenks is addressing often come from pairing learners with different abilities. There are good reasons to sometimes ask a stronger student to work with a weaker one, but doing so all the time risks frustrating both.

Two-way information gaps are the focus of Nakahama, Tyler, and van Lier (2001). They offer a critique of negotiation, specifically repair, as leading only to a focus on the words necessary to complete the interaction. They studied the interaction of three L1 Japanese intermediate English learners and three L1 English graduate students in linguistics. The subjects were given two tasks, one to spot the differences between two pictures (a classic information gap activity) and the other to have a conversation about their mutual interests.

Nakahama et al. found that there was more negotiation in the information gap activity but not significantly more (of course, the small numbers make the meaningful use of statistics difficult). The negotiation sequences were of different types, however. In the jigsaw task, pairs mostly negotiated words and phrases. In the conversation, pairs negotiated more general meanings, taking several A/B turns to do so. The quality of the interaction was also different. Speech in the jigsaw task was limited to short utterances; this was particularly true of the Japanese women:

> *Mindy:* . . . there's something—a rectangle with four dots?
> *Mayumi:* Yes.
> *Mindy:* You have that?
> *Mayumi:* Yes.
>
> (p. 390)

Compare that interchange with this more balanced one:

> *Mindy:* So what made you decide to get into journal-
> ism?
> *Mayumi:* Um, I think, uh, if I may be a journalist. . . .
> *Mindy:* Uh-huh
> *Mayumi:* . . . so I can work by myself. I mean, uh, I don't
> need to, uh, work for a company?
>
> (p. 391)

Conversations displayed grammatically more complex and varied language. Conversations were also more cohesive, while the information
gap exchanges were a series of small negotiating cycles. The cohesion in
them was simply local, one utterance connected to the last, with no
overall connections.

The researchers conclude that in an information gap situation,
learners are not pushed to produce language; they are pushed to produce a solution.

My feeling is that both kinds of activity are useful in the classroom,
but that much depends on the students and the situation. In second
language classrooms, students are motivated to learn and, generally
speaking, willing to participate. In foreign language classrooms, the
language is less real, requirements are often imposed from outside, and
motivation may not exist to participate in an unstructured conversation. I realize that's a gross generalization, and that there are plenty of
lively foreign language classrooms, but I say this only to point out the
importance of learning situation to task selection.

One aspect of motivation, and a perennial issue in pair work, is
how well students stay on track. Brooks, Donato, and McGlone (1997)
suggest that our conventional notions of task completion may not recognize that there are other, important opportunities for development
during the doing of the task. They looked at L1 English university
learners of Spanish as a foreign language doing jigsaw tasks. They
found that learners engaged in metatalk, talk about their own speech
such as, "Let me think of another way to say this" and "I like that
word" (p. 528). These statements increased over time (the subjects

completed five tasks) and tended to move from English to Spanish. Brooks et al. say that this metatalk is not superfluous or off-task, even in English. Instead, it helps students remain involved in the task and potentially helps them "notice the gap" in their abilities. The students also engaged in talk about the task itself. The amount of this talk decreased over time as they became used to doing information gap activities. Students overall made comments not just to their partners, but to themselves. They searched for words, whispered affective reactions, and mentally planned their next move. This increased interest and engagement and helps with task completion.

Brooks and his colleagues conclude by saying that we need to look at not just how messages are sent and understood, but "how forms of collaboration and social interaction unite the development of second-language orality with an individual's cognitive functioning" (p. 534).

Mondada and Pekarek Doehler (2004) argue for a revision of Vygotskian approaches like Brookes et al. They see interactional activities as not offering simply opportunities to solve problems and create learning, but also as part of the ways in "which members construct learning environments, tasks, identities, and contexts." In other words, tasks exist at a local level, but also in a wider context. Mondada and Pekarek Doehler admit that this position cannot be fully fleshed out in terms of "cognitive processes with any accuracy" at this time, but affirm that adopting their position could "radically" question distinctions between interior and exterior, individual and social (p. 515). I look at exterior and social next.

TABLE 28: Review of Interaction and Comprehension

Negotiated meaning is effective.	There is more to interaction than negotiated meaning.
Pica, Young, & Doughty (1987); Loschky (1994); Gass & Varonis (1994); Ellis, Tanaka, & Yamazaki (1994); He & Ellis (1999); Garcia and Ascención (2001)	Brooks, Donato, & McGlone (1997); Nakaham, Tyler, & van Lier (2001); Foster & Ohta (2005); Jenks (2009); Mondada and Pekarek Doehler (2004)

Social Factors in Listening ———

The act of listening looks like a matter between two individuals, but it exists in larger contexts, both societal contexts and classroom contexts. To my mind, the best source to begin to understand the larger societal context of listening is the European Science Foundation study of immigrant-gatekeeper interactions published as Bremer, Roberts, Vasseur, Simonot, and Broeder (1996). A "gatekeeper" is someone through whom another person must go to get services, in this case social services in a number of European countries. The overall study is centered on a "notion of understanding" as a "dynamic, public and cooperative activity in which both sides are actively engaged" (Roberts, 1996, p. 17). The study taped a number of interactions and then asked participants how they assessed the interaction.

Let's start with an example from Deulofeu and Taranger (1984) that is quoted by Roberts (1996, pp. 12–13). A Moroccan immigrant, Abdelmalek, goes to a travel agent in Marseilles to book a ticket from France back to Morocco. The agent asks how he wishes to travel. Abdelmalek mistakes *par quoi* (*how*) for *pourquoi* (*why*) and answers by saying that there are problems at home, his father is ill, and he has to leave right away. The agent is understandably confused. Abdelmalek later explained to the researchers that he was used to being interrogated by French people whenever he was in a formal situation, which he perceived the travel agency interaction as, so *why* made sense to him. Roberts points out it would not have made sense to a native French speaker, even though the words are close and can be confused because they do not have Abdelmalek's experience with the bureaucracy. This could be trivialized as an example of misplaced schema, or as lexical confusion, but it is a more powerful example than that. It shows that external social relations creep into everyday contexts.

Bremer (1996) looks at the causes for misunderstandings. There are those that can be attributed to singular causes such as not knowing or mishearing a word. There are also issues of complex utterances and ellipsis. To be sure, utterances are sometimes complex because the content necessitates an involved grammatical structure. But, as Bremer shows, sometimes complexity comes about as a result of the speaker being too polite (*I wonder if you come possibly, if it's not too much trouble, loan me a pen.*) if the topic or request is too intrusive. Speakers sometimes also over-explain. Gatekeepers do both, usually with the intention of giving respect to their clients. (I'd add that sometimes teachers do this to their students.) Elliptical utterances are also a problem. In these, the speaker leaves out information that is assumed known by the listener or over-uses pronouns, making connections within the discourse difficult. The listener cannot fill in the blanks. An example of ellipsis is this interaction between a dentist's receptionist and a patient (p. 62):

> T: fine and where do you live
> R: walsall
> T: what's the address sorry

The receptionist is asking for an address, assuming people go to the dentist in the town in which they live. The patient answers with the town's name, a perfectly good response to "Where do you live?"

Bremer (1996, p. 64) says that misunderstandings in the study sometimes "can be attributed to a kind of underlying misunderstanding with respect to defining features of the communication." In other words, each side misunderstands its relationship to the other, why questions are framed the way they are, what is expected.

At various places, Bremer et al. (1996) offer prescriptions for improved understanding that involve gatekeeper training as well as learner training. Gatekeepers need to learn to wait longer for answers rather than peppering their clients with too much elaboration. They need to more clearly mark new topics and keep on topic to make the conversation easy to follow. Learners need to take the initiative in order to control topics; they also need better inferencing skills. Both groups need to use feedback and clarification language and repetition more effectively.

Kasper (1997, p. 354) cautions that sometimes the strategies used by native speakers to achieve mutual understanding between themselves and non-native speakers can backfire and alienate the non-native speakers; they "may accentuate asymmetry and produce psychological divergence." Carrier (1999) further cautions that issues of social status may have an effect on listening comprehension.

Social relationships also play a role in classrooms. In classrooms, sometimes learners take on roles, and sometimes their roles are thrust upon them. Lynch (1997) offers a case study of Kazu, a Japanese student in a pre-academic program in Scotland. Lynch uses transcripts of class activities as well as listening tests to show Kazu's rather slow growth in listening. At the end of the short English course, Kazu's scores in one-way listening (comprehension of recorded audio) increased, but in regular coursework he struggled with two-way listening. Lynch shows how Kazu's status (relatively young, relatively less proficient) contributed to his problems in the intensive English courses. He also quotes Kazu as saying that his status as the only international student in his academic Economics classes made him feel that he couldn't negotiate meaning in them as readily as he did in his English classes. Lynch concludes that participation in academic seminars by language learners "requires fine interpersonal judgment as to how far you can tax your interlocutors' tolerance by asking for repetition, clarification and all the other things we recommend as good two-way listening strategies" (pp. 396–397).

An earlier study by Lynch (1995) looked at his pre-academic program's practice seminars, which required a traditional talk and questions from the floor, what Lynch calls a kind of "delayed negotiation" (p. 170). He shows how audience members, listeners all, had quite different roles. For example, he shows how audience members all participated to clarify the meaning of an example; he says "some learners in the group appeared to interpret their role of interactive listeners so positively that they also assisted other listeners to get their problems solved" (p. 177). Lynch concludes that we need to look at individual factors like perceptions of listening interactively, and non-participation, as well as social factors influencing interaction, such as relative authority/expertise and proficiency level.

Use of Strategies in Interaction ⎯⎯⎯

When speakers negotiate meaning, their efforts to make themselves understood can be see as "reception strategies." Most research on learner strategy use has been done on one-way, non-reciprocal listening to either recorded audio or the teacher, as we will see in Myth 8. Rost and Ross (1991) look at the use of strategies in interactive listening. They develop a typology of listener feedback moves during narratives told by a native English speaker to Japanese learners of English:

- **Global questioning**: asking for repetition or paraphrase of some part of the narrative, making some sort of verbal or non-verbal continuation signal indicating that the speaker can go on
- **Lexical questioning**: includes asking for lexical repetition or fragment repetition, asking the meaning of a word, and positional reprise (asking something about "the last part," for example)
- **Inferential strategies**: hypothesis testing (questions about some specific facts in the narrative) and formal inference (asking questions about given information in the text). Inferential strategies indicate some (perceived) understanding of the content of the narrative.

Rost and Ross found that more proficient learners used inferential strategies and less proficient learners used more local and global strategies. They then studied whether one of the moves, lexical clarification, was teachable. Subjects were taught to ask for lexical clarification when hearing a relatively complex story. Rost and Ross conclude that strategy use is essentially compensatory, so higher-proficiency learners do not need it as much as lower-proficiency learners do. However, lower-proficiency learners may get sidetracked by lexical clarification, if they choose to ask about words that they don't need for comprehension. Thus, lower-proficiency students need a full range of strategies. Rost and Ross also find that strategy use is constrained by the task and the interlocutor. At the simplest level, I take this to mean that there are situations where learners can't, or won't use strategies because of concerns about face (not wanting to bother another person). Kazu felt this way.

Vandergrift (1997b) modifies the framework of Rost and Ross somewhat, including coding separately for L1 and L2 responses and adding a specific kinesics category for feedback that consisted of shaking the head, waving arms, etc. Vandergrift studied the relationship of strategy use to oral proficiency level. He found that beginners depended on kinesics, global reprise (asking for repetition or paraphrase), and hypothesis testing (confirmation and clarification). Use of kinesics decreased with rise in proficiency level, even within beginners themselves. At the intermediate level, global reprise and hypothesis testing decreased and shifted from L1 English to the target language, French. At the intermediate level, there was more uptaking (back channeling like *Uh-huh*).

A more recent study by Farrell and Mallard (2006) sought to answer two questions: What types of reception strategies are used by learners of French engaged in an information gap activity in a Singapore classroom? Are there differences in use based on proficiency?

Students worked together in pairs to orally reconstruct a story about a drunk driving incident. Each member of the pair had ten cards with pictures. The 20 picture cards together told the story. The students couldn't see each other's cards. The interactions were taped, and the learners were interviewed after the task.

Farrell and Mallard discovered three categories of strategy use. The first is "strategies to develop new information." For example, listeners asked questions or made statements to check understanding. This they called "forward inference." The listener is moving the conversation forward by taking in new information, drawing a conclusion, and checking that conclusion. Also in the "develop new information" category is "uptaking" or back channeling. Finally, there was one case of "faking" in which the listener signaled uptaking when understanding would have been impossible because the partner used a non-existent word.

The second category is "strategies to confirm old information." This category includes hypothesis testing and text-level reprise.

Hypothesis testing for Farrell and Mallard means testing comprehension by repetition or paraphrase. Text-level reprise consists of repeating a word; Farrell and Mallard say that this indicates understanding at the sentence level but a lack of comprehension at a more global level.

The final category, clarifying old information, includes sentence-level reprise and global reprise. Sentence-level reprise indicates lack of comprehension on the sentence level, in other words confusion about words. Global reprise indicates lack of comprehension that is not specified (for example, a simple *huh?*).

In terms of proficiency, intermediate students used about three times more strategies than the beginners, and even more than the advanced students. The most used strategies were uptaking, hypothesis testing, and text-level reprise. All the other strategies were much less used. The infrequent use of most strategies and the relative non-use of strategies by lower-level students leads the researchers to call for more strategy training. Table 29 summarizes the reception strategies.

TABLE 29: Review of Reception Strategies in Interactive Listening

- ask for repetition of word, phrase, fragment, chunk
- ask for paraphrase, rephrasing
- ask for meaning of a word
- ask about "the first part," etc.
- non-verbal continuation signals
- non-verbal signs signaling lack of understanding
- verbal continuation signals, uptaking, back-channeling
- hypothesis testing: specific questions about the text to confirm understanding, rephrase of the text to confirm
- forward inference: specific questions about established facts
- repeating part of text, either to indicate understanding, or, with questioning intonation, lack of understanding
- indicate lack of global understanding (*huh?*)
- faking it: waiting to see if understanding emerges

Good Speaking Tasks ——

In this section, we will survey what is known about the "ideal" speaking task, realizing all the while that individual classrooms make such a thing elusive. There have been three important surveys of the elements of effective speaking tasks.

Pica and her colleagues (1993) surveyed the literature and concluded that tasks that promote comprehension, feedback, and interlanguage modification (all things we want) can be characterized by certain factors. They are: (1) a jigsaw structure in which each participant holds some information and must communicate it to a partner in a two-way interaction in order to successfully complete the task; (2) participants must have the same or convergent goals; and (3) there must be only one possible outcome to the task.

Keck et al. (2006), in a meta-analysis (a statistical procedure comparing studies, apples to apples) of 14 studies found relatively large effect sizes for interaction versus no interaction in speaking tasks. What does that mean? It means that tasks in which students interacted with each other led to gains in language learning. In terms of the kinds of tasks, jigsaw and information gap tasks (in which partners held different information) were seen to be particularly effective for language learning. Task-essentialness also seemed to be a very important factor; unfortunately, it is very difficult to build into tasks. Task essentialness means the learners are forced to use the structure the teacher wants them to use, as opposed to just saying *yes* or *the other one*. In real world communication, we do not speak in complete sentences or use very sophisticated grammatical structures in speech. We somehow need to give learners an opportunity to practice those in the classroom. This is a huge problem for materials developers. Mackey and Goo (2007) updated Keck et al. (2006), finding that interaction facilitated L12 development, even in delayed post-tests.

To the list of effective elements in speaking tasks we might also add pre-task planning and repetition of tasks (Ellis, 2005). Pre-task planning (giving students time to think about how they will perform the task) has been shown to increase fluency (students speak with fewer hesitations) and complexity of language (they are able to use more difficult structures). The results are mixed for accuracy, however, partially at least because as students use more complex structures, they sometimes make mistakes with them.

Task repetition is simply doing the task again. Most of us would think that students would become bored. But think about your own study of a foreign language. Wouldn't you have liked to work at something until you "had" it? Key to task repetition is changing partners so that the situation stays genuinely communicative. We can also engage in task cycles, in which the same language gets recycled in each step. A simple example of task repetition is to line up students in two lines facing each other. Give them two minutes to tell their partner three things they did last weekend. They will not be very fluent. Then their partner tells about the weekend. One partner moves to the right. The process begins again, except now they have 90 seconds to say the same thing. Change again, and now they have 45 seconds. The times are arbitrary, but the improvement in fluency will be significant. Lynch and Maclean (2001) have done an activity called "poster carousel" in which their professional students, who will be attending conferences and presenting in English, present a poster of their research to multiple partners individually. The students made significant gains in several areas.

In order to properly describe and sequence tasks, Robinson (2001) has argued that we need to take into account the cognitive demands tasks make on students, the interactive factors or participation variables, and learner factors.

This chapter has questioned our practice of thinking about listening as unidirectional. People interact with each other to make meaning. No matter how you characterize this interaction theoretically, or which parts of it you notice, it is as good or better for comprehension than any sort of linguistic modification. Meaning-making in dialogue deserves our scrutiny. We also need to think more about how society influences and indeed constrains that meaning-making.

What We Can Do . . .

1. Include speaking activities in class to provide opportunities for interactional listening.

Whether we accept the cognitive or sociocultural models of interaction, we believe interaction is a good thing. We may not agree with the other camp as to why that is or even how to organize interaction, but we all agree students need to talk to one another as well as to us. In the context of listening development, students need practice in conversation because they are going to be spending a lot more time (well, I hope more time) speaking to other people than listening to disembodied voices. We know quite a bit about how to organize speaking tasks, though of course there are disagreements about some of the details. Table 30 summarizes what I believe is good research on speaking tasks. I encourage you to keep these guidelines in mind when choosing or making your own tasks.

TABLE 30: Research on Speaking Tasks

1. **One-way vs. two-way tasks:** An example of a one way task is a story; an example of a two-way task is an information gap. In a two-way task, each partner holds a different portion of information that must be exchanged and manipulated to reach the task outcome. Two-way tasks lead to more negotiation of meaning.

2. **Closed vs. open tasks** (convergent/divergent): Closed tasks have only one acceptable outcome, and partners are forced to come to a conclusion. Closed tasks feature more topic and language "recycling," more feedback, and more precision.

3. **Shared goals:** Students can have same or convergent goals. It's best if they are trying to get to the same place.

4. **Pre-task planning:** This is effective in improving fluency and complexity of language. Results for accuracy are mixed.

5. **Repetition of the task:** This can be effective with a different partner or partners.

6. **Consider the cognitive and task demands:** Is the task appropriate for your learners in terms of what it asks them to do? (Repetition may help here.)

2. Use a variety of speaking tasks.

We have already looked at a variety of listening tasks. Here, I want to give you some idea of the variety of speaking tasks that are possible. Given the disagreements over specific kinds of tasks, I think it makes sense to use a wide variety of tasks and get the best of all worlds. I'm going to start by organizing some very basic activities that any teacher or class can do into Brainstorming Tasks and Problem-Solving Tasks, even though there is overlap between them. First, however, I want to enunciate three principles:

1. Students must know how to say what they want to say. This implies doing a pre-speaking task to activate knowledge of the topic or to pre-teach vocabulary. It also implies, for me at least, some kind of support on the board (if it's not in the textbook); this usually takes the form of stems of sentences, phrases that students might need to successfully complete the task. You can't anticipate every problem, but you can anticipate useful language that will smooth the completion of the task.

2. Students must have a goal. Teachers get frustrated when they (or the textbook) says, *Discuss* or *Talk about . . . ,* and nothing happens. Why should anything happen? What are students supposed to do? Give them a goal: Find three things they both did last weekend. Giving a task a goal gives it a target, something to move toward and focus on.

3. Students must be motivated to do the task. I'm not saying that there isn't a certain amount of hard work that must go into language learning, but if students are talking about things that matter (their lives) or things that are enjoyable (puzzles, games), they are more likely to want to work hard at the task.

BRAINSTORMING TASKS

- Finding connections: Students make connections between pictures, each other, etc. The main task is to link two (or more) things. This could be telling a story that incorporates a number of pictures, or uses a number of words.
- Things that are the same: Students find three to five similarities and/or differences between people, cities, etc.
- Explaining: The teacher explains possible uses for odd items or uses pictures to guess what happened before or will happen.
- ABC Game: Groups work to think of an item beginning with each letter of the alphabet, in order, repeating the previous ones. Teacher or last person points to the next participant. There is no writing.
- Chalkboard race: Teams line up and, individually, in turn, write examples of categories that the teacher calls out, in a given time.

PROBLEM-SOLVING TASKS

- Odd one out: Given three to five choices, students work together to find the one that doesn't belong, and give reasons why.
- Differences: Students find differences between two pictures or cartoons. The children's section of the newspaper often has these sorts of puzzles.
- Ordering: Students put pictures in order to tell a story. Order strip stories, individual sentences or paragraphs that form a story.
- Prioritizing: The teacher selects candidates for a job or selects the most or the best anything.
- Find someone who . . . : The teacher writes on the board, dictates, or gives out a list. (e.g., *Find someone who likes cats*). Students must find a member of the class

that can answer *yes* to each item on the list. Once a person answers *yes*, that person can't be used again. However, as many questions as necessary can be asked to get a *yes*.

- Combining: Students work with another group and share the results of the task. Decide which is the better solution. Combine results, and cut the list to the top two or three.

3. To make interaction more effective, teach reception strategies.

Students need to be taught reception strategies at a practical level appropriate to given tasks—not all at once and abstractly. If a task requires them to write something, make sure they know the phrase, *How do you spell that?* If the task is an information gap, they need *Could you repeat that, please?* Strategies need to be available for the learners in the classroom, on the board, or, if possible, on a poster on the wall. Table 31 shows some ideas to get you started.

TABLE 31: Feedback Language for Interactive Listening

- Could you repeat that, please?
- Once more, please.
- Did you say X?
- Did you say X or Y?
- Do you mean X?
- I don't understand.
- I didn't hear you.
- Can we start again?
- I'm lost.
- OK. Got it.
- What's next?

7

MYTH

Students should listen only to authentic materials.

In the Real World . . .

I was listening to the Grateful Dead's *American Beauty* one day after working on this book (I *do* listen to new music, too, but sometimes a beautiful Great Lakes spring afternoon requires perspective). My brain hadn't shut down the "listening research" network yet, so I, much against my will, experienced sporadic connections between the songs on the album and the topic of listening. It began with the line in "Sugar Magnolia" that compares a woman's dancing to "a Willys in four-wheel drive." Leaving aside the aptness of the comparison, I began to wonder how many of my Ohio-born students knew what a Willys was (the original Jeep). Then "Operator" came on, in which the singer is seeking a phone number. How many young people have spoken to a telephone operator?

Though this music is 40 years old, it's still on sale. It's "authentic." But it might as well be written in Martian. Perhaps I'm being perverse, but what would happen if you tried to present this authentic material in class, or if a language learner found it at a yard sale? What schema is activated by the word *operator*? If you had students write down everything they knew about operators or Willys, how far would you get? You could go the bottom-up route and look up the words in a bilingual dictionary, but I doubt proper names of defunct car companies would be there, and I wonder about the telephone meaning of operator. (I think of the confused look on the face of my Japanese student who had found the circular-area meaning of circus—Piccadilly Circus—and not the tents and elephants one.)

The issue of authenticity in materials has plagued language teaching for decades. In staff rooms in Asia and the United States, I've heard colleagues declare that they would only teach with authentic materials. They scorned textbooks as contrived, unrealistic. They spent enormous amounts of time scouring newspapers and magazines for authentic articles. In the pre-Internet era, expatriate teachers had friends send videocassette tapes of television programs and movies from home.

I, too, have tried to use authentic materials when I can. I forget where we got them, but in 1980s Tokyo we had homemade tapes of the TV shows *Miami Vice* and *Family Ties* we used for listening practice. A couple of years ago while living in Taiwan, I bought a *Friends* DVD at the local video store to show in the last classes. I think authentic materials have a definite place in language teaching, but I think often that place is mostly about motivation. Students, at least some students, like to see the cultural products of the languages they are studying, especially if those products (movies, TV) are designed for and feature characters the same age as they are. In some cases, attaining the ability to consume popular culture is why people are studying a foreign language. For example, many Americans like Japanese *anime* and *manga* (animation and comic books) and study Japanese largely to be able to understand them. Students in Asia learn Japanese or Korean to understand pop music from those countries. Some students, however, really don't care about the target culture; they are more interested in using English to speak to other English learners than to native English speakers, in using English as an International Language.

Though I recognize that understanding authentic material is a goal most students have, I don't think we are well served by a rigid insistence that all classroom materials be authentic and I'd like to look at that issue in this chapter. I want to note that this chapter comes out of a joint presentation and subsequent thinking and revising I have done over the years with my former colleague at the University of Pittsburgh, Lionel Menasche (Brown & Menasche, 1993).

What the Research Says . . .

Authenticity in materials design and learning activities has never been far from the thoughts of ELT professionals. Indeed, several positive effects have been claimed to flow from such authenticity, among them: increased student motivation due to face validity (the material *looks* real and is therefore exciting), provision of appropriate cultural knowledge, exposure to "real" language, attention to future student needs, and support of more creative teaching (Richards, 2001, pp. 252–253).

Authenticity has been an important feature of communicative approaches to language teaching. Somewhere along the way, for some people at least, providing authentic materials to students has become a moral issue. Clarke refers to the "elevation of 'authentic' materials to the level of what appears to be a categorical imperative" (1989, p. 73), a moral necessity. Mishan notes that "authenticity is a positive attribute, collocating with desirable qualities such as purity, originality and quality" (2004, p. 219).

Tomlinson states that there are typically two sides in this debate: "One side argues that simplification and contrivance can facilitate learning; the other side argues that they can lead to faulty learning and that they deny the learners opportunities for informal learning and the development of self-esteem" (2003, p. 5). Presenting a balanced position, he also says,

My own view is that meaningful engagement with authentic texts is a prerequisite for the development of communicative and strategic competence but that authentic texts can be created by interactive negotiations between learners. . . . I also believe, though, that for particularly problematic features of language use it is sometimes useful to focus learners on characteristics of these features through specially contrived examples. . . ." (Tomlinson, 2003, p. 6).

We might say that historically there have been three common positions:

1. The strong authenticity position: language is best learned if all input is authentic.
2. The non-authenticity position: language is best learned if all input is specially written for the learners.
3. The intermediate authenticity position: language is best learned if input is varied in degree of authenticity according to the learner's proficiency and the purpose of the lesson at that point in the curriculum.

Various definitions have been offered for authenticity, the most common being a perhaps over-simplified one that is based on the original intention of the writer or speaker: anything produced expressly for language learning is not authentic, while anything uttered for any other purpose is authentic. Thus, "Texts are said to be authentic if they are genuine instances of language use as opposed to exemplars devised specifically for language teaching purposes" (Johnson, 1998, p. 24).

Yet authenticity is not an easy concept to pin down. Dunkel (1995, p. 98) points out that terms like *authentic language, authentic discourse,* and *authentic materials* are all defined in "holistic, vague, and imprecise ways." Widdowson early in this debate claimed that authenticity is not inherent in texts but is found in "the act of interpretation" (1979, p. 165). That is, it is a measure of reader or listener response. This claim has raised the issue "authentic for whom"—the teacher, the learner, or the materials writer (Breen, 1985)?

Later, Widdowson (1998) has elaborated his critique of the notion of authenticity. His argument is that learners are outside the community that originally authenticated the text; therefore "the language that is authentic for native speaker users cannot possibly be authentic for learners" (p. 711). However, the language can become authentic for learners through the learning process if that process addresses their interests, attitudes and cultural contexts, "not those of the unfamiliar foreign community whose language they are learning but whose reality they are in no position to relate to" (p. 714). This argument seems to me to refer more to EFL contexts, in which the relevance of the target culture is indeed often not great. In ESL contexts, things become a bit murkier, as issues of accommodation to the wider community surface. We don't want to deny learners access to the majority culture, nor do we want to demand total assimilation. Ultimately, Widdowson is talking about the process of acquiring language, however, and less about the goals.

Despite the difficulties in defining authenticity, researchers and teachers have seemed to know it when they see it. Though much of the literature on authenticity is prescriptive or theoretical, there have been a few empirical studies, which can be broken down into the following categories: comparisons between authentic materials and classroom materials, studies of the efficacy of authentic materials, and suggestions of how technology can help access authentic materials.

Textbooks vs. Real Life ———

Gilmore (2007) reviews a number of features of authentic language not found in classroom materials and concludes that textbooks typically offer decontextualized language. Gilmore especially recommends material that provides visual as well as aural context. In an earlier study (Gilmore, 2004), he compared seven service encounters from ESOL textbooks to real-life encounters that he simulated from the questions he extracted from the textbook dialogues. Each of the real conversations was nearly twice as long as the textbook conversation it was based on; real life interlocutors asked for more details (in booking a hotel room, for example), and there were more alternatives. There was greater lexical density in the textbooks; that is, there were more content words in the fabricated conversations, making them more like written than spoken language. False starts, repetition, pauses, and overlap in speaking were all more frequent in real life.

Crossley, Louwerse, McCarthy, and McNamara (2007) used the computer tool Coh-Metrix to analyze seven beginning-level ESOL textbooks, only two of which included authentic texts. (Of course, beginning-level books are not likely to include authentic materials). The authentic and "simplified" texts were compared on the basis of syntactic features. (I have a problem with their use of "simplified" because it means to me the adaptation of an authentic source, making the language simpler, rather than the production of an original simple text, and there are no indications exactly how the writers of the materials they studied in fact produced what they called "simplified.") The authentic texts had more features of causal language, more cause-effect structures, more word types (parts of speech), and lower frequency words. The simplified texts relied on repeated nouns and pronouns and simple conjunctions for connecting the discourse together. The authors point out that the effect of simple texts is choppy sentences, which in turn are difficult to process, because the learners wind up having to supply their own connections between sentences.

Roberts and Cooke (2009) used discourse analysis to compare textbook dialogues to real-life service encounters such as doctor-patient conversations. They advocate using corpora collected from real-life in classrooms to make students aware of cultural scripts and hidden power arrangements.

There have been a number of other studies that have compared textbooks to real language (see Table 32 on page 138).

TABLE 32: Selected Studies on Authentic and Textbook Conversations

Conversational closings	Surveyed textbooks and found most of their dialogues did not feature the complete structure of closings.	Bardovi-Harlig et al. (1991)
Complaints and commiseration	Textbooks teach a small subset of complaints and do not convey the appropriate use of commiseration.	Boxer & Pickering (1995)
Conversational closings	Neither textbooks nor TV soap operas always follow research-based findings on patterns of closings, but soap operas are useful for language learning.	Grant & Starks (2001)
Phone conversations	Textbook conversations did not resemble the typical structure of telephone conversations found in research.	Wong (2002)

Do Authentic Materials Help Listening? ——

Studies have claimed that authentic listening materials are effective in the classroom (there have been more studies of authentic reading materials). Herron and Seay (1991) studied the effects of the addition of authentic radio programs to classes for American university French learners. One class spent a little more than one-third of class time listening in a structured way (with pre-listening and teacher support between listenings) to a French radio program, while another class spent that time reviewing grammar and vocabulary and practicing oral skills. Both classes used the same video-based course the rest of the time. The students who listened to the authentic materials did better on listening tests and did as well as the other students on tests of grammar, vocabulary, and oral skills, though they didn't have extra study in them, as the control group did.

Materials produced by native speakers of German were rated highly in terms of authenticity and usefulness for learning by American students learning German; authentic listening produced some anxiety (Chavez, 1998).

Weyers (1999) reported that viewing an authentic *telenovela* (a Spanish-language soap opera) increased university students' listening comprehension, confidence, and number of words and amount of detail they used in a subsequent speaking task over a control group that didn't watch the video (though not to a statistically significant degree).

Crandall and Basturkmen (2004) taught requests by asking students to analyze materials drawn from a corpus of university-based requests. Students were surveyed and reported that they found the authentic materials useful for learning and enjoyable to use. A pre-test/post-test design revealed that the materials were in fact effective; students improved in their abilities to produce native-like requests. In conclusion, use of authentic materials in listening classes has been shown to be effective in increasing comprehension and also might help with acquisition of other skills. Students also enjoyed using authentic materials.

Authenticity and Technology ——

Recently, researchers have advocated the connection of technology to use of authentic materials in the classroom. Their efforts seem to imply that authentic materials are best used with mediation or help. Mishan and Strunz (2003) used an XML application to develop an online teacher resource that generates pedagogical tasks to accompany authentic materials, based on discourse types. Meinardi (2009) used a tool that slows down authentic speech to increase comprehension. Robin (2007) points out that, with technology, authentic materials are repeatable and easily modified, and that this is an authentic use of the materials as well, for native listeners also take advantage of these tools. Robin says that the notion that you have only one chance to listen is no longer true, given the availability of digital video recorders (DVRs) and downloadable clips from sites like You Tube: "In short, *listening has become a semi-recursive activity, less dependent on transient memory*, inching its way closer to reading, which is fully recursive" (p. 110, italics in original). Robin also mentions (1) software for slowing speech delivery, (2) captioning, (3) transcripts on news sites, (4) translation bots that might serve to give beginning listeners the main idea and some details, and (4) interactive chat as potential helpers for second language listeners.

A Model of Authenticity: Text, Task, and Output ——

You may believe that you owe your students authentic materials. However, I'm asking your consideration of a model that tries to place authenticity on a continuum. I hope this model helps you think about authenticity and how it applies to your classroom.

I think we need a model that distinguishes input authenticity, task authenticity, and output authenticity. I believe we need to account for several degrees of authenticity because authenticity is not a binary (either-or) concept and because in practice complete authenticity is impossible to achieve in the classroom—and here, by "complete," I mean authenticity measured in terms of all three elements: input, task, and output, each of which can be complex in the classroom and in materials. There are types and degrees of each, and the types and degrees can be combined in various ways, creating overall teaching episodes that are difficult to characterize in a simple way as authentic or inauthentic.

Types of Input Authenticity ——

Input is the text (written or spoken) that is read or heard by the learner. I think there are at least five types of input authenticity. I am explicitly rejecting the word *level* to avoid the implication that one type is better than any other. The five types are:

1. *Genuine input authenticity:* The input is created only for the realm of real life, not for the classroom, but is used in language teaching. No changes at all are made in the text. Examples: An entire movie watched without interruption and without consulting the script. This is how we experience movies in real life.

2. *Altered input authenticity*: There is no meaning change in the original input, but it is no longer exactly as it was because of changes like lexical glossing (marginal or footnoted definitions), visual resetting, or changes in pictures or colors, in the case of reading. Example: A movie shown in five-minute segments, with vocabulary work and discussion following each segment.

3. *Adapted input authenticity*: The input is created for 'real life' but adapted by the classroom teacher. Words and grammatical structures are changed, usually to simplify the text (e.g., difficult words are changed to synonyms or glossed). This category also covers the case of elaboration, in which a text is expanded to make it more comprehensible to learners. Examples: In terms of listening, a teacher might re-record a news segment in order to simplify it. The effect is most clearly seen in graded readers of literary classics, in which, for example, *Jane Eyre* is rewritten within a 500-word vocabulary.

4. *Simulated input authenticity*: The input is created for the classroom and attempts to copy the style and format of the genuine. It is written by the author or teacher *as if* the material were real and *as if* for a real audience. It may have many authentic text characteristics and is often indistinguishable from the genuine. Example: A listening textbook with conversations that sound as if they could have been overheard.

5. *Inauthenticity*: The input is created for the classroom with no attempt to make the materials resemble genuine authentic materials, though there may be a few, possibly incidental, authentic features. However, it should be emphasized that "inauthenticity" does not imply that such materials are of lesser pedagogical worth than those that are genuine, altered, adapted, or simulated. Examples: Timed readings with apparatus for learners to time themselves and note their progress,

grammar exercises, input for pronunciation practice (e.g., minimal pair words), and formal explanations of grammatical points.

Types of Task Authenticity ——

The idea of input is perhaps more central to our topic of listening, but the idea of task is also important to listening instruction.

Perhaps the most commonly cited definition of task has been Nunan's (1989, p. 10) formulation: "a piece of classroom work which involves learners in comprehending, manipulating, producing or interacting in the target language while their attention is principally focused on meaning rather than form." I will define *tasks*, for purposes of this model, somewhat more narrowly as "what learners do with input."

In offering the following typology of task authenticity, I admit there is probably no such thing as real task authenticity, that classrooms are by their nature artificial. The only genuine task authenticity for language learning may well be total immersion in the target language environment without an instructor. Nevertheless, I'm going to argue that there are three types of task authenticity: genuine, simulated, and pedagogical.

1. *Genuine task authenticity* exists when learners engage in tasks in ways and for reasons they would in the real world.
2. In *simulated task authenticity*, there is some attempt to copy the real within the context of the classroom, but the focus is on language learning.
3. *Pedagogical task authenticity* occurs when there is no attempt to copy the real, but the task is useful within the context of the classroom.

Consider the example of reading a newspaper editorial. The genuinely authentic task would be to read the article silently and move on to reading another article without imposed discussion or language exercises. This would be considered inappropriate in a classroom, unless there was time assigned for sustained silent reading, and even then, if the learner would have rather read a magazine than the newspaper, the purpose is language learning and so the task is not genuinely authentic. Simulated task authenticity would apply, for example, to an activity in which learners are paired and must imagine themselves to be roommates discussing the editorial. In this, there is some attempt to copy the real world. Another common task with simulated authenticity would be one in which the instructor requires the learner to write a letter to an editor to comment on an actual editorial. Pedagogically authentic tasks include answering comprehension questions about the editorial, comparing two editorials on one subject and listing the similarities and differences, and then writing a composition on the topic of the editorial.

Thus, we have an interaction between input authenticity and task authenticity. Examples are given as Table 33 on page 144, in the form of a two-dimensional grid showing input type and task type.

TABLE 33: Typical Classroom Events Characterized by Input and Task
<u>Note</u>: In principle, output authenticity will vary by individuals.

	Genuine Task	Simulated Task	Pedagogical Task
Genuine Input	Learners watch an L2 movie or read for pleasure.	Learners use a newspaper to role-play roommates discussing the news.	Learners outline an article in a newspaper.
Altered Input	Learners watch an L2 movie or read for pleasure, but with supporting glosses to explain idioms.	Learners watch an L2 movie with supporting glosses for idioms, then role-play the characters.	Learners answer comprehension questions about an annotated, photocopied article.
Adapted Input	Learners read a simplified classic novel (graded reader) for pleasure.	Learners all read the same simplified classic novel (graded reader) and discuss it.	Learners answer comprehension questions in a simplified classic novel (graded reader).
Simulated Input	Learners read a simulated article in a textbook because they are interested in the topic.	Learners decide which restaurant to eat at, based on simulated advertisements in a textbook.	Learners answer questions in a reading textbook containing simulated readings.
Inauthentic Input	Inauthentic material does not lend itself readily to genuine tasks.	Learners do pronunciation practice in the context of a scripted dialogue.	Learners complete a pair work activity about imaginary people.

Types of Authentic Output ——

Output refers to the product of a task, the language actually used or spoken. I differentiate two kinds of authentic output based on the criterion of communicative reality, in hopes of addressing the issue of response raised by Widdowson (1979).

1. *Genuine output:* This is based on the learner's actual beliefs or personal knowledge, conveying what the learner thinks is real or true information. Examples: contributions to class discussion or essays.

2. *Simulated output:* This is essentially all the rest, in which the learner is not communicating information that is personally believed or known. Examples: performance of a role play or the repetition of a sentence in a pronunciation exercise.

Authenticity is not a moral issue. It is a teaching issue. Sometimes it's useful, and sometimes it's not. Ultimately, students need all different kinds of input.

What We Can Do . . .

1. Use technology to provide practice with authentic materials.

Weren't we supposed to have household robots and commute to work in hovercraft by now? The promise of technology has frequently been just that—a promise. In language learning, though, we definitely have progressed from the reel-to-reel tapes of my high school, which, of course, no one could take home, to the Internet. I'm not entirely convinced that the Internet changes a great deal of what we do as language teachers, and that's not its job; its job is providing videos of cats playing the piano. In fact, the Internet offers lots of material for listening, to both conversations and longer narrative.

It's always difficult to provide the URLs of websites in books, which are revised infrequently, if ever, while sites change all the time. I am going to assume everyone is proficient at web searches by now and will offer simply a list of good websites that you can access through your favorite search engine.

First, let's look at websites that are not designed for language learners. All the major news organizations (ABC, NBC, CBS, CNN, Fox) offer a wide variety of material, including segments from their news programs and, frequently, extra interviews. Students are supported (somewhat) by the pairing of video and sound (though actually more often than not the voice-over does not match the visuals, which can be confusing). The interviews are especially good because they pair body language with sound. The BBC World Service and National Public Radio (NPR) are radio-based, so offer only sound and still photography (but overall somtimes higher quality).

Voice of America is somewhat in the middle between programming for native English speakers and programming for language students. It understands its audience may not have English as its first language, but it still offers a challenge to students. It also has programs in Special English. Special English uses a 1,500-word vocabulary, short sentences and is spoken at a slower rate than standard English.

Perhaps more fun than the news is You Tube. TV commercials are short and often very clever. Students should search for "funny commercials." There are also many music videos with lyrics on You Tube. To get lyrics, type the name of the song or artist and "lyrics." Lyrics can also be found at music.yahoo.com. Episodes from sit-coms are also available on the web (and on DVD); sit-coms are only about 23 minutes long, so they make good organized lunch activities. (Thanks to Marc Helgesen for these ideas.)

There are numerous sites for learning English, but among those dedicated solely to listening, Randall's ESL Cyber Listening Lab and English Listening Lounge probably offer the most; the latter asks for a small fee. The site for *English Firsthand*, www.efcafe.com, includes video versions of the course dialogues called Drama Coach, as well as short narratives with cloze passages. The Internet TESL Journal (iteslj.org and a4esl.org) has podcasts geared to students. I've recently become aware of eslfolk.com, which has lessons plans built around American folk songs.

The educational sites offer tasks, but the news organizations do not. You could use the list of listening tasks in Myth 4 to construct worksheets focusing on different skills, or could use a simple report form, like this, that students could hand in to show that they had done work outside of class.

Listening Report

Name:

What I listened to:

How long I listened:

Three things I learned:

1.

2.

3.

Students could also use this form to report video (movie or TV) viewing. Alternatively, you could ask video viewers to make up a short, five-question quiz about the video they watched and they could then challenge their classmates to watch the video and take the quiz. For songs, students could write five to ten lines from the song in random order and challenge their classmates to put the lines in the correct order. The same task could be done with individual words, or (if the students like to draw) with pictures.

Mishan (2004) encourages the use of corpora. Though corpora do not present language in its original context, students can "authenticate" the corpora by engaging in data-driven learning, using concordance programs to help them formulate definitions and work on collocations. Translation: Corpora are collections of texts containing millions of words. Concordance programs allow anyone to find regularities in the data by selecting words or phrases. All instances of a word or phrase are lined up, and once lined up can be seen in typical environments. From there, generalities can be constructed, and definitions and collocations (typical combinations of words) made.

2. Adapt tasks to learners' abilities.

Those who have encouraged the use of authentic materials have adopted the slogan *Grade the task, not the text*. This means that in principle we can use any text, no matter how difficult, so long as we require an appropriate response from learners, one that matches current level of proficiency with cognitive demands of the task. At the beginning level, in principle, we could use a newscast and ask how many stories there were. Students would only have to understand when the topic changed. I'm not sure anyone would find this entirely satisfactory, however, in terms of motivation or perhaps even in terms of true comprehension.

Nevertheless, we often adapt texts to meet the realities of the classroom. As we have seen, students may have problems with speech rate, unfamiliar words, unfamiliar pronunciation of familiar words, stress, intonation, and grammatical structures. They may have difficulties with the topic, the organization of the text, or the kind of text. I have stressed the importance of pre-tasks to overcome, or at least lessen, some of these difficulties. To adapt texts, we typically rewrite them in simplified language, elaborate them with extra information, allow students to negotiate their meaning, or perhaps simply repeat them with no change, with the teacher reading instead of the audio, or with a change of stress or speed.

Tasks can also be difficult when they make too many demands on learner knowledge or ask learners to do too many things at once. The level of response may be too high; what is asked of students may be beyond their productive ability. The response time may require students to be quicker than they are. To adapt tasks, break them into steps, and do a class feedback session at each step before moving on in order to find what the difficulties are (see Table 34). Limit responses to checking a box or writing a word, as opposed to formulating sentence responses to comprehension questions. Use a limited number of task types, so students don't have to complete the task and learn how to do it at the same time. List key words or example sentences on the board to guide students. Find related pictures on the Internet and use them to help comprehension. Provide a script—sometimes, but not all the time.

TABLE 34: Review of Making and Texts and Tasks Easier

Texts	Tasks
• Rewrite/re-record	• Break into steps with feedback sessions between
• Give extra information	
• Use pre-tasks	• Limit response
• Ask students to work together	• Use limited number of task types
• Repeat with or without modifying speed	• Provide key words and example sentences
• Read the transcript	• Use pictures to illustrate
• Provide script	

Listening can't be taught.

In the Real World . . .

This story is from my friend Dorolyn Smith (she of the health/home story in Myth 2): The new car I bought a year ago came with a free trial of satellite radio. Flipping through the stations, I discovered Radio Quoi de Neuf, a French Canadian news station.

My background: My French study consisted of two years in high school, a year in college (French 2 & 3), and a couple of visits now and then to France—over the past 30 years. Although my study was more than 40 years ago, I can "get by" as a tourist in France. However, I am a fairly sophisticated language learner: I am an ESL teacher with an MA in linguistics, speak good Spanish and Portuguese, and have studied or speak a couple of other languages in varying degrees of proficiency. I'm a language-learning geek.

I started to listen to Quoi de Neuf every day for a few minutes when I first got my car. What fascinated me was that I didn't understand a single thing—although I can speak conversational French OK. I could tell it was French but couldn't segment words. In fact, I didn't even realize that they were repeating the same three-minute news cycle over and over! But after about a week of just letting Canadian French wash over me, I caught the words *la presse canadienne*, so I started to listen for that. Two days later, I caught *les informations de la presse canadienne*. Now I had something to hang onto, and two days later I caught this phrase: *Voici les informations de la presse canadienne*. I realized that if that was a beginning, there might be a closing with something like *c'etait . . .* , and sure enough, that day I listened for and heard *C'etait les informations de la presse canadienne*. I was so excited because now I knew what I was listening to and for: a short news cycle with a beginning and an end. The next time I listened, I heard the announcer's name: *Ici Claude de Fornier. Voici les informations de la presse canadienne*. Now I was making a new discovery each time I listened. The very next time, I heard the real clue to the beginning of the cycle, the greeting: *Bonjour Mesdames et Messieurs, ici Claude de Fornier. Voici les informations de la presse canadienne*. A few days later, I heard the expression *dans le monde de sport . . .* and came to learn that sports was always the last item of the cycle. Soon I was able to distinguish different news items even if I didn't understand the topic.

I continue to tune in every day to Quoi de Neuf, just to see what I can understand. I can always segment news items, and I know when someone is being interviewed for a report. Sometimes I understand only a detail, sometimes I get the main idea; often I get the topic but not the main idea of the topic. I understand much of the sports news. I know most of the announcers by name. I know the different ways of varying the pronunciation of *Voici les informations de la presse canadienne* by changing the intonation, stress, and pauses.

I often imagine myself as an announcer on Quoi de Neuf and practice introducing myself and the news. It is one of my minor dreams in life to be on radio and able to say *"Bonjour Mesdames et Messieurs, ici Dorolin Smeet. Voici les informations de . . . la presse canadienne."*

Dorolyn was applying strategies she has acquired as a life-long language learner. This chapter is about strategies and the debate over their use in language teaching and learning. If you're new to the field, you might want to consult the What We Can Do section (pages 161–64) for an overview of stategies.

What the Research Says . . .

Strategies help organize learning. They also allow learners to out-perform their current competence, to compensate for things they don't know. O'Malley and Chamot (1990) presented what has come to be an influential way of looking at strategies, dividing several different kinds of strategies into three broad categories: cognitive, meta-cognitive, and social/affective strategies. Cognitive strategies, like note-taking and guessing words from context, facilitate learning. Meta-cognitive strategies are those that help students organize and reflect on their learning. Some meta-cognitive strategies are planning and monitoring of comprehension (thinking while listening to see if the details that are accumulating make sense in the bigger picture). Social/affective strategies include those that facilitate getting input from other people and are relevant mostly in interactive listening. A major issue for teachers and researchers has been the proliferation of strategies, which has come about as a result of rather loose definitions (Ridgway, 2000). Field (2000) notes the confusion between learning strategies, which are more general, and compensatory strategies, which are used when the learner has a shortage of resources and must fill a gap in skills or knowledge. Examples of learning strategies are note-taking and memorization. Examples of compensatory strategies are guessing word meaning in context and circumlocution, talking around an unknown word so that the listener understands the meaning without the word itself being used. Field also warns against teaching strategies as products chosen from a list. He notes that the success rates for this kind of strategy teaching are ambiguous, partially because of the difficulties in testing listening improvement and partially because of the difficulty students have using strategies in real time.

Research into strategies has settled around two questions. Does strategy use improve listening comprehension? What strategies do successful listeners use?

Does Strategy Use Improve Comprehension? ⸻

One thread of strategy research has claimed that teaching students to use strategies will improve their listening comprehension. These studies have tended to be short-term, from a few hours to at most a year. Most have followed students over a semester. It is not common to follow up after students leave the class, to see if the training is used outside the classroom. Typically, students are tested on their listening ability, receive training, and then are re-tested.

Vogely's (1995) study combines a number of questions, including images of a good listener, the strategies students use, and the relationship between strategy use and listening comprehension scores. The research looked at 83 U.S. university students of Spanish. Since it was a small university, students in their first, second, and third semesters were all studied. Students were given a standardized listening test and a meta-cognitive awareness survey. Then they watched or listened to three episodes of a Spanish language TV program. Students were highly aware of listening strategies but didn't use all of them. They used some effective strategies, like trying to get the gist, relating background knowledge to what is heard, and focusing on details. They also tried to understand the meaning of every word, which was probably not so effective (strategies can be ineffective as well as effective). There was much going on in this study, but overall, there was a positive correlation between strategy use and listening comprehension scores. That is, more strategy use led to better comprehension. There was also an interesting finding that all groups performed less well when they couldn't see the visuals of the program and had to rely only on sound, which backs up research we've seen throughout the book on the power of visuals.

Vogely's study did not explicitly teach strategies, though students must have known them from previous classes because they did exhibit a high degree of knowledge in the strategy questionnaire. Thompson and Rubin (1996) explicitly taught cognitive and meta-cognitive strategies to one group of third-year Russian students at a U.S. university. Their listening comprehension scores were compared to a group that received no strategy training; instead, this group did speaking and writing activities. Both groups had a video component to class. Cognitive strategies taught included predicting content, making use of background knowledge, listening for redundancies and to tone/intonation, and writing words and phrases. Meta-cognitive strategies taught were planning, defining goals, monitoring, and evaluating. Also, genre-specific strategies were taught: focusing on the storyline in a drama; paying attention to the question-and-answer sequence in an interview; and thinking about five questions (*who, what, when, where, how*) when listening to the news. There were two tests, one video-based and the other audio-based. Students who received strategy training made significant gains on the video test. Gains on the audio test were not significant, perhaps because the test contained genres that were not in the training videos or because pre-test scores on this test were high so there was less room for growth. Students reported using a variety of strategies in out-of-class listening, such as watching with the sound off the first time to get the gist of a video or turning the picture off in the second listening of newscasts because the incongruity of sound and picture could be distracting. They also reported generally being able to understand what to listen for in a second listening.

Taiwanese junior college students were assigned two required in-class and two out-of-class tasks of their own choice per week and reflected on them through listening journals and interviews (Chen, 2007). There were explicitly taught strategies: getting the gist, keyword, selective attention (focus), using context, grouping, inferring, elaborating (using prior knowledge, relating it to the text to fill in missing information and predict), self-monitoring, and imaging. Students reported that, upon completion of the program, they were comfortable with texts of greater complexity; paid more attention to strategy use; were more focused and organized when they listened; were able to choose strategies to use, and used strategies in reading and writing as well; and remembered more of what they had listened to. They claimed their proficiency improved; some mentioned that a local English language radio program that had been too fast now seemed slow.

Many strategy training studies begin with a list of strategies culled from the research literature. Graham and Macaro (2008) began with a needs analysis. They found that adolescent learners did engage in prediction before listening tasks, but this was largely a matter of looking at the answers to multiple choice questions. This strategy focused them on individual words, which they then listened for, largely without thinking about the larger context. Also, they did not consider that the audio might contain not the exact words from the answers, but rather synonyms for those words. To the extent they used prior knowledge, they listened through it to impose their ideas on the text, rather than using prior knowledge to understand the text.

Given this knowledge, Graham and Macaro (2008) focused on teaching predicting, confirming predictions, identifying key words, inferring, recognizing familiar words, and separating words in the speech stream. They conceptualized the strategies as interconnected, not a list to be applied serially and separately. There were two experimental groups, which differed in the amount of scaffolding they received for the training, and one control group, which received no strategy training. The high scaffolding group (HSG) used a strategy diary, written feedback on strategy use, and group discussions; the attempt was to organize a higher degree of reflection about the training, compared to the low scaffolding group (LSG). There was a pre-test, an immediate post-test, and a delayed post-test six months later. Strategy training overall was found effective in both post-tests. At the time of the first post-test, HSG outperformed LSG (and both outperformed the control group). At the time of the second post-test, both groups again tested better than the control group, but LSG outperformed HSG. The authors say that this was likely due to a particularly high rate of attrition among LSG; the best and most motivated learners were likely to remain. When asked their perception of the process, more of the HSG overall, compared to the other two groups, felt they had improved in listening, though the difference was not significant.

Graham and Macaro (2008) were also interested in whether strategy training would lead to greater self-efficacy, to learners being more confident in their abilities. Both experimental groups had higher gains in self-efficacy scores than the control group, but the differences were not significant.

Cross (2009) did not find any difference between two groups of Japanese adults given either 12 hours of strategy instruction or none. Both groups made gains in a video-based program. Cross points out that the two classes behaved very differently in terms of interaction, though, which points out that the atmosphere of the classroom influences everything.

In a study of Canadian university high-beginning and lower-intermediate learners of French (Vandergrift & Tafaghodtari, 2010), learners were taught a process that combines and coordinates a number of strategies (see also Vandergrift 2003a, 2003b). The process led to improved comprehension overall, compared to a control group. Lower-proficiency students were helped the most. The differences in improvement scores of higher-proficiency students in both the experimental and control groups were not statistically significant (though, again, the experimental group as a whole did better than the control).

Do strategies develop over time, with proficiency, if not explicitly taught? Graham, Santos, and Vanderplank (2008) presented a longitudinal study of two students selected from a group of 15. Their strategy use did not change much over six months, though the lower-proficiency student did make some change from focusing on individual words in listening to trying to chunk words. The higher-proficiency student, compared to the lower-proficiency student, used more comprehension monitoring and vocalized the words he heard.

Goh (2008) has surveyed instruction in meta-cognitive strategies and has concluded that they improve listening comprehension, especially for less proficient listeners. She further claims that their use makes students more confident and more motivated. However, she urges a move from thinking about meta-cognitive strategies in isolation to thinking about the larger issue of metacognition and metacognitive knowledge: personal knowledge (knowledge of self as listener); task knowledge (understanding the nature of listening); and strategy knowledge (knowledge of when to apply strategies). Goh has also argued (2002) for a conceptualization of strategies that sees each strategy subsuming a number of tactics.

A dissent about the efficacy of teaching strategies is offered by Renandya and Farrell (in press). Their argument is that strategy training has not been shown to be effective, that it takes up a lot of class time, and that it requires expertise that many teachers do not have. Therefore, they urge adoption of an extensive listening program that combines teacher dictations, teacher read-alouds and listening-while-reading, self-directed listening and narrow/repeated listening. Renandya and Farrell are implicitly supported in their comment that strategy training requires teacher development by an advocate of strategies, Chamot (1995). Chamot (p. 25) focuses much of her survey of strategy research on teacher development issues and concludes by saying that while strategy instruction has been shown to improve listening comprehension, "numerous difficulties have been encountered in instructional design and teacher preparation."

Table 35 summarizes the research.

TABLE 35: Review: Does Strategy Use Improve Comprehension?

Yes
Vogely (1995), Chamot (1995), Thompson & Rubin (1996), Chen (2007), Goh (2008), Graham & Macaro (2008), Vandergrift & Tafaghodtari (2010)
No
Cross 2009, Renandya & Farrell (in press)

What Strategies Do Successful Listeners Use?

Many of the studies that tell us which strategies successful listeners use begin as more general studies of the efficacy of teaching strategies, while others begin with comparing more and less skilled listeners. At the very beginning of strategy research in language teaching, O'Malley, Chamot, and Küpper (1989) stressed the importance of meta-cognitive strategy use. They found that effective listeners used self-monitoring, elaboration, and inferencing skills. Skilled listeners among the Hispanic secondary students they observed stayed on track, processed larger chunks, used context to infer, and related what they knew to what they heard. In other words, they processed top-down.

Unsuccessful listeners listened word-by-word and stopped listening when they heard unfamiliar words.

In a comparison of more and less successful listeners in university Spanish classes, Bacon (1992) noted that successful listeners were motivated to look up new words after listening. They knew more details and thus were more precise in their summaries. They elaborated on and connected to their background knowledge. Less successful listeners relied too much on their background knowledge and therefore came up with erroneous interpretations and were bothered by unfamiliar vocabulary.

High school learners of French in Canada (Vandergrift, 1997a) overall used more cognitive strategies than meta-cognitive strategies. However, strategy use differed with proficiency. Meta-cognitive strategy increased with proficiency; intermediate students used more meta-cognitive strategies than beginners. They used planning, comprehension monitoring, self-evaluation, and problem identification. Conversely, intermediate students used fewer cognitive strategies like repetition, translation, and other types of transfer from L1. When the comparison was between successful and unsuccessful listeners, the biggest difference was in the use of meta-cognitive strategies, especially comprehension monitoring and problem identification. There were fewer differences in cognitive strategy use between the successful and unsuccessful, except in the use of translation, which was a strategy that the unsuccessful tended to use.

Higher-proficiency Taiwanese learners used cognitive strategies like inference and the ability to connect new information to known. They were able to make use of repeated words in the text to form a solid representation of its meaning (Chien & Wei, 1998).

In a case study done in Singapore with two students from China who were studying English, Goh (2002) reported that the more proficient student used more strategies and tactics, but both the higher- and lower-proficiency students used top-down processing when possible. Both got stuck at certain points but were able to keep listening.

Vandergrift (2003a) reported in his study of junior high school students learning French in Canada that there was a significant difference in meta-cognitive strategy use by higher-skilled students, who used comprehension monitoring and questioning elaboration (combining questions to self with prior knowledge). They applied world knowledge to think about the logical possibilities for what they were hearing, interpreted what they heard, and then formed a frame of reference, which they constantly updated. Less-skilled listeners used translation strategies.

Berne's (2004) review of listening strategy research concluded that more proficient listeners use strategies more often, use a wider range of strategies, and use them interactively, which is to say in combination. Skilled learners are more aware of text structure and attend to larger chunks of text than less skilled listeners, who tend to listen word by word. She also concluded that good listeners monitor their comprehension and, in the process, relate what they hear to previous experiences. According to Berne, less proficient learners work at the word level, rely on translation and individual key words, make fewer inferences, and don't relate what they hear to what they know.

Table 36 summarizes some strategies and why they are effective.

TABLE 36: Condensation of Macaro, Graham & Vanderplank (2008, p. 750): Strategies Consistently Seen as Important to Listening

Strategy	Why Effective
Predicting content of text	Lightens processing load by lowering possibilities; utilizes schema
Selective attention for certain words/phrases/ideas	Confirms, disconfirms predictions
Monitoring comprehension, checking for correct interpretation	Ties everything together
Use linguistic context, background information clues to infer meaning of unknown words	Compensates for what is lacking

Finally, Macaro (2006) questions the theoretical framework of language learning strategies. He locates strategies in working memory and says they must work in clusters (see Goh, 2008, and Vandergrift, 2003a, for clustering strategies). He further claims that social/affective strategies are really part of metacognition.

Rost (2002) argues for the importance of these teachable strategies:

- predicting information
- inferencing
- monitoring comprehension
- clarifying/asking for clarification
- responding to what has been heard in an interactive situation
- evaluating how well you have done

TABLE 37: Methodology: Think-Alouds

Many times, studies of strategies use some sort of student reflection to get at what students were thinking and which strategies they used. Interaction or an individual task might be taped and then students would view the video and say what they were thinking. Ideally, the student would do this in L1. It is also possible to do this online. Students can listen and tell what they are thinking as they are listening. This is perhaps more difficult, particularly with lower-proficiency students, as they are being asked to do a lot at the same time. While some researchers question the use of think-alouds—sometimes because they believe that it's very difficult to get at what listeners are really doing—this technique is widely used.

Strategies have proliferated over the past 30 years, until sometimes it seems like everything is a strategy. At the same time, strategies have become a kind of magic wand for breaking through language learning barriers and delivering proficiency. We've seen that strategies can be effective, but they're not magic. Useful and necessary, yes, but not magic.

What We Can Do . . .

1. Work to develop strategies for listening.

While the trend is to think about strategies as clusters rather than as discrete items taught serially, it makes some sense to enumerate the individual strategies before clustering them, and to present them as they have been presented since O'Malley and Chamot (1990). Here is a list of strategies to get you thinking about how you might use them in your classroom.

Cognitive strategies are ways for students to organize their own learning. Here are some cognitive strategies that are used in listening:

- taking notes
- guessing words in context
- using knowledge of language such as grammatical structures, stress, intonation, discourse markers, and individual words, particularly to fill in gaps in comprehension
- using schemata and knowledge of the topic to predict what will be heard, and to predict what is next
- using knowledge of the situation and context to narrow down possible meanings
- making links between what is heard and the topic and making links between prior knowledge and the topic
- making inferences
- making use of non-verbal cues in conversation

Meta-cognitive strategies help students organize their listening. These are some meta-cognitive strategies involved in listening:

- pay attention and focus while listening
- check understanding
- identify problems
- adjust listening plan based on new information
- tie together, extend, and elaborate meaning
- monitor understanding
- develop an overall sense of what is heard, a storyline

Social/affective strategies are those concerned with interactive listening. Here are a few:

- seek practice opportunities
- find ways to get input
- deal with motivation
- deal with anxiety
- use clarification and confirmation language
- understand speaker reasons and motivations

The list of pre-listening activities I developed early in the book is implicated in teaching strategies. Here is the list again (see Table 38), with the strategies it encourages referenced.

TABLE 38: Tasks and Strategies

Pre-Listening Task	Strategies for More Effective Listening
What's the topic? Write five things you know about the topic.	Use knowledge of the topic to develop a plan for listening and to update your plan as you listen.
Look at the word list. Check the words you know.	Use knowledge of words and grammatical structures to develop knowledge of the topic. Use this knowledge as you listen to guess meaning in context.
What's your purpose for listening? Circle it.	Identify your purpose for listening before listening and update it as you listen.
Look at instructions. What's the situation?	Use instructions to figure out your purpose for listening. Use your purpose as you listen to check your understanding.
Look at the pictures. Write words.	Use what is on the textbook page to help you find the topic.
Look at the choices you have.	Use your choices to listen for specific words.
Now make a LISTENING PLAN. Think about: what you know; your answers to the questions given here; what you will FOCUS on.	Make a plan: what will you listen for? Update this plan as you listen.

If you are going to teach students how to listen in addition to giving them listening practice, you will need to use pre- and post-listening tasks. Ideally, you would be able to see how students are using strategies as they listen. But that is, of course, impossible, except in individual cases, using think-aloud protocols. So, in order to get some sense of how students are listening, you will need to stop after each playing of the audio to discuss how the students are responding, what difficulties they are having, and what they need to do next. It's often a good idea to stop after the first item, if there are several, and check the answer, just to see if everyone is comfortable and knows what they are doing. You then finally need to have a wrap-up session to see how their plans worked. Table 39 is a sample of what might be done after each playing of the audio. You might want to let the students work in pairs to do this step, as they will likely hear different things and might be able to give each other hints for the next time or benefit from discussing differences. After this step, you might consider one of Richards (2005) "listening for acquisition" activities (Myth 4).

TABLE 39: Monitoring Understanding

After the First Listening 1. What was easy? 2. What was difficult? 3. What do you need to find out in the next listening? **After the Last Listening** Was your plan useful? Circle one. Yes No Why?

Finally, a word about wrong answers. They offer insight into your students' listening processes. It is possible that your pre-listening activities will lead students down the wrong path. Schemata may be activated improperly, so that learners impose preconceptions on the material. Be alert to evidence of this in their answers (answers that are wildly off topic). Also be aware that they may be missing details because they are relying on the vocabulary on the page and not actively thinking about synonyms or linking knowledge to form inferences. If they get off track, model your own comprehension of the passage; talk about the schemata you are bringing, the connections you are building, and the guesses you are making.

2. Use a variety of assessment techniques.

We have looked throughout this book at attempts to improve listening. The attempts have been tested in various ways, both quantitatively and qualitatively. Of course, in our classrooms we are constantly evaluating student improvement. When we think about listening tests, many of us probably think about standardized tests with multiple choice questions; several of the studies used these sorts of tests. These are discrete point tests; in fact, any test that tests a particular aspect of a listening passage and scores it right or wrong can be considered a discrete point test. There are other kinds of tests and assessments, however, and we should branch out and use a variety of them.

Integrated tests include written or spoken summaries of a text, clozed (fill in the blanks) summaries of a text, and dictation. The integration comes from the whole-text approach.

Performance-based tests ask students to perform a task that they might do in the real world, such as write down information they received over the phone. This might lead to a speaking or writing activity.

Interview tests can feature the teacher and the student, or two students interacting. Students answer questions. The questions may vary in authenticity. ACTFL (the American Council on Teaching Foreign Languages) has been a leader in interview testing. The organization's standardized approach leads to a designation relative to a native speaker of the language.

Self-assessments ask students to rate their own abilities on a list of criteria. Students may also assess their proficiency in written or spoken journals. Self-assessment can provide part of the material in a portfolio, which covers the entire course and includes several different measures of proficiency.

Conclusion

I've given a lot of presentations to teachers, and I think I'm always careful to spell out the implications of the research I talk about. But not infrequently on feedback forms or in face-to-face conversations after, teachers want to know what it means for *their* classroom, and pointing out that I teach in *my* classroom, not *their* classroom, does not seem to satisfy them. In this book, I've tried to be as practical and explicit as I can be, but you will need to take these ideas and fit them to your classroom. I haven't focused on teaching children because there's simply not a lot of research out there on L2 children's listening. I haven't gone into academic listening as deeply as I could have. I wanted to speak more generally about listening. But you're smart people. I'm sure you can see your students in these pages, and use the book's ideas to make them better listeners.

I began by questioning the idea that reading and listening are identical. While they may share many processes, the fact that speech and writing are different ultimately means that reading and listening are dissimilar. While readers, working with a fixed text, are able to remember more ideas and more details, listeners, working with fleeting sounds, get a more global understanding. They also rely more on background knowledge to make meaning.

Background knowledge was the focus of Myth 2. Listeners actively utilize what they know about a topic to help comprehension. Research has tried to find the right kind of pre-listening activity. Several kinds have been found to be effective, but much depends on the proficiency of the students and the task they have to accomplish. Use of schemata to understand what we hear shows that listening is active. Each listener, rather than receiving meaning, creates meaning.

Comprehension has been at the center of much listening research, but Myth 3 showed that there is more to listening than comprehension.

Characteristics of speech like assimilation, elision, and insertion change the sounds of words that students have learned in isolation, often making them unrecognizable. Word recognition is also affected by the processes we use to understand our native languages, processes that don't work when applied to other languages.

Word recognition is one of many factors in listening difficulty. Myth 4 surveyed several. Prescriptions for improving comprehension have included better lexical knowledge, slower speech rates, effective pauses, and elaboration of the message. All except lexical knowledge depend on the speaker, so listeners need ways to take control of the conversation and give the speaker useful feedback.

Not all listening is two-way, however, Myth 5 reminded us that students need to hear different kinds of input, including videos and lectures, where appropriate. New kinds of dictation (especially dictogloss, which takes advantage of longer texts) can be effective in teaching language forms and their extended use seems to be effective for developing comprehension skills.

Myth 6 looked at the social aspects of listening, from pairs talking together to the constraints that students feel in classrooms and, because of social roles, within society at large.

Myths 7 and 8 surveyed two, to my mind, over-hyped answers to the question of how we improve learners' language. One prescription has been to use authentic materials, but we've seen no consensus on defining just what "authenticity" is. I offered another model. Another prescription has been strategy training. While strategy use is one piece of the learning puzzle, it's not, to my mind, even the biggest piece. I do think that meta-cognitive/meta-linguistic training offers some ideas that are very important, however.

Finally, listening is challenging because it is meaning-making, and that's a process that is difficult to view directly. I noted at the beginning of this book that writers frequently bemoan the lack of research on listening. By now, you're probably thinking that there's been too much. We do have more to do to understand listening, but you'll probably agree that there *is* much we know, and much of it is relevant to the classroom. It remains for teachers to buck the myths, think hard about listening, and apply or adapt the ideas they find most useful for their classrooms.

References

Absalom, M., & Rizzi, A. (2008). Comparing the outcomes of online listening versus online text-based tasks in university level Italian L2 study. *ReCALL 20*, 55–66.

Adams, R. (2007). Do second language learners benefit from interacting with each other? In A. Mackey (Ed.), *Conversational interaction in second language acquisition: A collection of empirical studies* (pp. 29–51). Oxford, U.K.: Oxford University Press.

Adolphs, S., & Schmitt, N. (2003). Lexical coverage of spoken discourse. *Applied Linguistics 24*, 425–438.

Alderson, J.C. (1984). Reading in a foreign language: A reading problem or a language problem? In J.C. Alderson, & A.H. Urquhart (Eds.), *Reading in a foreign language* (pp. 1–24). London: Longman.

Alderson, J.C., & Urquhart, A.H. (1977). *Reading in a foreign language*. London: Longman.

Al-jasser, F. (2008). The effect of teaching English phonotactics on the lexical segmentation of English as a foreign language. *System 36*, 94–106.

Anderson, A., & Lynch, T. (1988). *Listening*. Oxford, U.K.: Oxford University Press.

Anderson, R.C. (1994). Role of the reader's schema in comprehension, learning and memory. In R.B. Ruddell., M.R. Ruddell, & H. Singer (Eds.), *Theoretical models and processes of reading, 4th edition* (pp. 469–482). Newark, DE: International Reading Association.

Anderson-Hsieh, J., & Koehler, K. (1988). The effect of foreign accent and speaking rate on native speaker comprehension. *Language Learning 38*, 561–613.

Bacon, S.M. (1992). Phases of listening to authentic input in Spanish: A descriptive study. *Foreign Language Annals 25*, 317–333.

Bardovi-Harlig, K., Hartford, B.A.S., Morgan-Taylor, R., Morgan, M.J., & Reynolds, D.W. (1991). Developing pragmatic awareness: Closing the conversation. *ELT Journal 45*, 4–15.

Bartlett, F.C. (1932). *Remembering*. Cambridge, U.K.: Cambridge University Press.

Bent, T., & Bradlow, A.R. (2003). The interlanguage speech intelligibility benefit. *Journal of the Acoustical Society of America 114(3)*, 1600–1610.

Berkleyen, N. (2009). Helping teachers become better English students: Causes, effects, and coping strategies for foreign language listening anxiety. *System 37*, 664–675.

Berne, J.E. (1995). How does varying pre-listening activities affect second language listening comprehension? *Hispania 78*, 316–329.

Berne, J.E. (2004). Listening comprehension strategies: A review of the literature. *Foreign Language Annals 37*, 521–533.

Blau, E.K. (1982). The effect of syntax on readability for ESL students in Puerto Rico. *TESOL Quarterly 16*, 517–528.

Blau, E.K. (1990). The effect of syntax, speed, and pauses on listening comprehension. *TESOL Quarterly 24*, 746–753.

Block, D. (2003). *The social turn in second language acquisition.* Washington, DC: Georgetown University Press.

Bonk, W.J. (2000). Second language lexical knowledge and listening comprehension. *International Journal of Listening 14*, 14–31.

Boyle, J.P. (1984). Factors affecting listening comprehension. *ELT Journal 38*, 34–38.

Boxer, D., & Pickering, L. (1995). Problems in the presentation of speech acts in ELT materials: The case of complaints. *ELT Journal 49*, 44–58.

Breen, M.P. (1985). Authenticity in the language classroom. *Applied Linguistics 6*, 60–70.

Bremer, K., Roberts, C., Vasseur, M., Simonot, M., & Broeder, P. (Eds.). (1996). *Achieving understanding: Discourse in intercultural encounters.* London: Longman.

Bremer, K. (1996). Causes of understanding problems. In K. Bremer, C. Roberts. M. Vasseur, M. Simonot, & P. Broeder (Eds.). *Achieving understanding: Discourse in intercultural encounters* (pp. 37–64). London: Longman.

Brett, P. (1997). A comparative study of the effects of the use of multimedia on listening comprehension. *System 25*, 39–53.

Broersma, M., & Cutler, A. (2008). Phantom word activation in L2. *System 36*, 22–34.

Brooks, F.B., Donato, R., & McGlone, J.V. (1997). When are they going to say 'it' right? Understanding learner talk during pair work activity. *Foreign Language Annals 30*, 524–541.

Brown, G. (1995). *Speakers, listeners and communication: Explorations in discourse analysis.* Cambridge, U.K.: Cambridge University Press.

Brown, G., & Yule, G. (1983). *Teaching the spoken language: An approach based on discourse analysis of conversational English.* Cambridge, U.K.: Cambridge University Press.

Brown, J.D., & Hilferty, A. (1986). The effectiveness of teaching reduced forms for listening comprehension. *RELC Journal 17*, 59–70.

Brown, R., Waring, R., & Donkaewbua, S. (2008). Incidental vocabulary acquisition from reading, reading-while-listening, and listening to stories. *Reading in a Foreign Language 20*(2), 136–163.

Brown, S., & Menasche, L. (1993). Authenticity in Materials Design. TESOL Conference. Atlanta, Georgia, 16 April 1993.

Brown, S., & Smith, D. (2007). *Active Listening 1.* New York: Cambridge University Press.

Buck, G. (2001). *Assessing listening.* Cambridge, U.K.: Cambridge University Press.

Bygate, M., Skehan, P., & Swain, M. (Eds.). (2001). *Researching pedagogical tasks: Second language learning, teaching and testing.* Harlow, U.K.: Longman.

Carrell, P. (1987). Content and formal schemata in ESL reading. *TESOL Quarterly 21*, 461–481.

Carrier, K. (1999). The social environment of second language listening: Does status play a role in comprehension? *Modern Language Journal 83*, 65–79.

Celce-Murcia, M., Brinton, D.M., Goodwin, J.M., with Griner, B. (2010). *Teaching pronunciation: A course book and reference guide.* Cambridge, U.K.: Cambridge University Press.

Cervantes, R., & Gainer, G. (1992). The effects of syntactic simplification and repetition on listening comprehension. *TESOL Quarterly 26*, 767–770.

Chamot, A.U. (1995). Learning strategies and listening comprehension. In D.J. Mendelsohn, & J. Rubin (Eds.), *A guide for the teaching of second language listening* (pp. 13–30). San Diego: Dominie Press.

Chang, A. C-S. (2007). The impact of vocabulary preparation on L2 listening comprehension, confidence and strategy use. *System 35*, 534–550.

Chang, A. C-S. (2009). Gains to L2 listeners from reading while listening vs. listening only in comprehending short stories. *System 37*, 652–663.

Chang, A. C-S., & Read, J. (2006). The effects of listening support on the listening performance of EFL learners. *TESOL Quarterly 40*, 375–394.

Chang, A. C-S., & Read, J. (2007). Support for foreign language listeners: Its effectiveness and limitations. *RELC Journal 38*, 375–395.

Chaudron, C. (1983). Simplification of input: Topic restatements and their effects on L2 learners' recognition and recall. *TESOL Quarterly 17*, 437–458.

Chaudron, C. (1988). *Second language classrooms: Research on teaching and learning*. Cambridge, U.K.: Cambridge University Press.

Chaudron, C. (1995). Academic listening. In D. Mendelsohn & J. Rubin (Eds.), *A guide for the teaching of second language listening* (pp. 74–96). San Diego: Dominie Press.

Chaudron, C., & Richards, J.C. (1986). The effect of discourse markers on the comprehension of lectures. *Applied Linguistics 7*, 113–127.

Chavez, M.M.T. (1998). Learners' perspectives on authenticity. *IRAL 36*, 277–306.

Chen, Y. (2007). Learning to learn: The impact of strategy training. *ELT Journal 61*, 20–29.

Chiang, C.S., & Dunkel, P. (1992). The effect of speech modification, prior knowledge, and language proficiency on EFL lecture learning. *TESOL Quarterly 26*, 345–374.

Chien, C-N., & Wei, Li. (1998). The strategy use in listening comprehension for EFL learners in Taiwan. *RELC Journal 28*, 66–91.

Chung, J-M. (1999). The effects of using video texts supported with advance organizers and captions on Chinese college students' listening comprehension: An empirical study. *Foreign Language Annals 32*, 295–308.

Chung, J-M. (2002). The effects of two advance organizers with video texts for the teaching of listening in English. *Foreign Language Annals 35*, 231–241.

Clarke, D.F. 1989. Communicative theory and its influence on materials production. *Language Teaching 22*, 73–86.

Clerehan, R. (1995). Taking it down: Notetaking practices of L1 and L2 students. *English for Specific Purposes 14*, 137–155.

Conrad, L. (1989). The effects of time-compressed speech on native and EFL listening comprehension. *Studies in Second Language Acquisition 11*, 1–16.

Crandall, E., & Basturkmen, H. (2004). Evaluating pragmatics-focused materials. *ELT Journal 58*, 38–49.

Crookes, G., & Gass, S.M. (1993). *Tasks and language learning: Integrating theory and practice*. Clevedon, U.K.: Multilingual Matters.

Cross, J. (2009). Effects of listening strategy instruction on news videotext comprehension. *Language Teaching Research 13*, 151–176.

Crossley, S.A., Louwerse, M.M., McCarthy, P.M., & McNamara, D.S. (2007). A linguistic analysis of simplified and authentic texts. *Modern Language Journal 91*, 15–30.

Davis, P., & Rinvolucri, M. (1988). *Dictation: New methods, new possibilities.* Cambridge, U.K.: Cambridge University Press.

Day, R., & Bamford, J. (1998). *Extensive reading in the second language classroom.* Cambridge, U.K.: Cambridge University Press.

DeKeyser, R.M. (2001). Automaticity and automatization. In P. Robinson (Ed.), *Cognition and second language instruction* (pp. 125–51). Cambridge, U.K.: Cambridge University Press.

Derwing, T.M. (1996). Elaborative detail: Help or hindrance to the NNS listener? *Studies in second Language Acquisition 18*, 283–297.

Derwing, T., & Munro, M.J. (2001). What speaking rates do non-native listeners prefer? *Applied Linguistics 22*, 324–337.

Deulofeu, J., & Taranger, M. (1984). Relations entre le linguistique et le culturel-microscopie de quelques malentendues et incomprésensions. In C. Noyau, & R. Porquier (Eds.), *Communiquer dans la langue de l'autre* (pp. 99–129). Paris: Presses Universitaries da Vicennes.

Dörnyei, Z. (2005). *The psychology of the language learner: Individual differences in second language acquisition.* Mahwah, NJ: Lawrence Erlbaum Associates.

Dörnyei, Z., & Kormos, J. (1998). Problem-solving mechanisms in L2 communication: A psycholinguistic perspective. *Studies in Second Language Acquisition 20*, 349–385.

Dunkel, P.A. (1995). Authentic second/foreign language learning texts: Issues of definition, operationalization, and application. In P. Byrd (Ed.), *Material Writer's Guide* (pp. 95–106). New York: Heinle and Heinle.

Dunkel, P., & Davis, J.N. (1994). The effects of rhetorical signaling cues on the recall of English lecture information by speakers of English as a native or second language. In J. Flowerdew (Ed.), *Academic listening: Research perspectives* (pp. 55–74). Cambridge, U.K.: Cambridge University Press.

Dupuy, B.C. (1999). Narrow listening: an alternative way to develop and enhance listening comprehension in students of French as a foreign language. *System 27*, 351–361.

Ehrlich, S., Avery, P., & Yorio, C. (1989). Discourse structure and the negotiation of comprehensibile input. *Studies in Second Language Acquisition 11*, 397–414.

Ellis, R., Tanaka, Y., & Yamazaki, A. (1994). Classroom interaction, comprehension, and the acquisition of L2 word meanings. *Language Learning 44*, 449–491.

Ellis, R. (Ed.). (1999) *Learning a second language through interaction.* Amsterdam: John Benjamins.

Ellis, R. (Ed.). (2005). *Planning and task performance in a second language.* Amsterdam: John Benjamins.

Elkhafaifi, H. (2005a). The effect of prelistening activities on listening comprehension in Arabic learners. *Foreign Language Annals 38,* 505–513.

Elkhafaifi, H. (2005b). Listening comprehension and anxiety in the Arabic language classroom. *Modern Language Journal 89,* 206–220.

Erickson, F. (1986). Listening and speaking. In D. Tannen & J.E. Alatis (Eds.), *Languages and linguistics: The interdependence of theory, data, and application (Georgetown University Round Table on Languages and Linguistics, 1985)* (pp. 294–319). Washington DC: Georgetown University Press.

Farrell, T.S.C., & Mallard, C. (2006). The use of reception strategies by learners of French as a foreign language. *Modern Language Journal 90,* 338–352.

Field, J. (2000). 'Not waving but drowning': A reply to Tony Ridgway. *ELT Journal 54,* 186–195.

Field, J. (2004). An insight into listeners' problems: Too much bottom-up or too much top-down? *System 32,* 363–377.

Field, J. (2008a). *Listening in the language classroom.* Cambridge, U.K.: Cambridge University Press.

Field, J. (2008b). Bricks or mortar: Which parts of the input does a second language listener rely on? *TESOL Quarterly 42,* 411–432.

Field, J. (2008c). Revising segmentation hypotheses in first and second language listening. *System 36,* 35–51.

Flowerdew, J. (1994). Research of relevance to second language lecture comprehension—An overview. In J. Flowerdew (Ed.), *Academic listening: Research perspectives.* (pp. 7–33). Cambridge, U.K.: Cambridge University Press.

Flowerdew, J., & Miller, L. (1992). Student perceptions, problems and strategies in second language lecture comprehension. *RELC Journal 23*(2), 60–80.

Flowerdew, J., & Tauroza, S. (1995). The effect of discourse markers on second language comprehension. *Studies in Second Language Acquisition 17,* 435–458.

Flowerdew, J., & Miller, L. (1996). Lecturer perceptions, problems and strategies in second language lectures. *RELC Journal 27*(1), 23–46.

Flowerdew, J., & Miller, L. (1997). The teaching of academic listening comprehension and the question of authenticity. *English for Specific Purposes 16,* 27–46.

Flowerdew, J., Miller, L. & Li, & David C.S. (2000). Perceptions, problems and strategies in lecturing in English to Chinese-speaking students. *RELC Journal 31*(1), 116–138.

Folse, K. (2004). *Vocabulary myths: Applying second language research to classroom teaching.* Ann Arbor: University of Michigan Press.

Foster, P., & Ohta, A.S. (2005). Negotiation for meaning and peer assistance in second language classrooms. *Applied Linguistics 26*, 402–430.

Garcia, P. (2004). Pragmatic comprehension of high and low level language learners. *TESL-EJ 8(2)*, 1–15. Retrieved from http://www.tesl-ej.org/wordpress/issues/volume8/ej30/ej20a1. Accessed July 21, 2010.

Garcia, P., & Asención, Y. (2001). Interlanguage development of Spanish learners: Comprehension, production, and interaction. *Canadian Modern Language Review 57*, 377–401.

Gass, S.M. (1997). *Input, interaction, and the second language learner.* Mahwah, NJ: Lawrence Erlbaum.

Gass, S.M., & Varonis, EM. (1994). Input, interaction, and second language production. *Studies in Second Language Acquisition 16*, 283–302.

Gilbert, J. (1995). Pronunciation practice as an aid to listening comprehension. In D.J. Mendelsohn, & J. Rubin, R. (Eds.). *A guide for the teaching of second language listening* (pp. 97–112), San Diego: Dominie Press.

Gilmore, A. (2004). A comparison of textbook and authentic interactions. *ELT Journal 58*, 363–374.

Gilmore, A. (2007). Authentic materials and authenticity in foreign language learning. *Language Teaching 40*, 97–118.

Ginther, A. (2002). Context and content visuals and performance on listening comprehension stimuli. *Language Testing 19*, 133–167.

Goh, C. (2000). A cognitive perspective on language learners' listening comprehension problems. *System 28*, 55–75.

Goh, C.C.M. (2002). Exploring listening comprehension tactics and their interaction patterns. *System 30*, 185–206.

Goh, C. (2008). Metacognitive instruction for second language listening development: Theory, practice and research implications. *RELC Journal 39*, 188–213.

Graham, S. (2006). Listening comprehension: The learner's perspective. *System 34*, 165–182.

Graham, S., & Macaro, E. (2008). Strategy instruction in listening for lower-intermediate learners of French. *Language Learning 58*, 747–783.

Graham, S., Santos, D., & Vanderplank, R. (2008). Listening comprehension and strategy use: A longitudinal exploration. *System 36*, 52–68.

Grant, L., & Starks, D. (2001). Screening appropriate teaching materials: Closings from textbooks and television soap operas. *IRAL 39*, 39–50.

Grgurovic, M., & Hegelhemier, V. (2007). Help options and multimedia listening: Students' use of subtitles and the transcript. *Language Learning & Technology 11*, 45–66. Retrieved from: http://llt.msu.edu/vol11num1/grgurovic. Accessed June 19, 2010.

Griffee, D. (1982). *Listen and act: Scenes for language learning.* Tokyo: Lingual House.

Griffiths, R. (1992). Speech rate and listening comprehension: Further evidence of the relationship. *TESOL Quarterly 26*, 385–390.

Griffiths, R. (1990). Speech rate and NNS comprehension: A preliminary study in time-benefit analysis. *Language Learning 40*, 311–336.

Guichon, N., & McLornan, S. (2008). The effects of multimodality on L2 learners: Implications for CALL resource design. *System 36*, 85–93.

Harris, T. (2003). Listening with your eyes: The importance of speech-related gestures in the language classroom. *Foreign Language Annals 36*, 180–187.

Hasan, A.S. (2000). Learners' perceptions of listening comprehension problems. *Language, Culture and Curriculum 13* (2), 137–153.

He, X., & Ellis, R. (1999). Modified output and the acquisition of word meanings. In R. Ellis (Ed.), *Learning a second language through interaction* (pp. 115–132). Amsterdam: John Benjamins.

Helgesen, M., & Brown, S. (2007). *Practical English language teaching: Listening.* New York: McGraw-Hill.

Helgesen, M., Brown, S. and Wiltshier, J. (2010). *English firsthand access.* Hong Kong: Pearson Longman.

Henrichsen, L.E. (1984). Sandi-variation: A filter of input for learners of ESL. *Language Learning 34*, 103–126.

Herron, C.A., & Seay, I. (1991). The effect of authentic oral texts on student listening comprehension in the foreign language classroom. *Foreign Language Annals 24*, 487–495.

Herron, C., Hanley, J.E.B., & Cole, S.P. (1995). A comparison study of two advance organizers for introducing beginning foreign language students to video. *Modern Language Journal 79*, 387–395.

Hoven, D. (1999). A model for listening and viewing comprehension in multimedia environments. *Language Learning & Technology 3(1)*, 88–103. Retreived from: http://llt.msu.edu/vol3num1/hoven. Accessed June 19, 2010.

Hulstijn, J.H. (2003). Connectionist models of language processing and the training of listening skills with the aid of multimedia software. *Computer Assisted Language Learning 16*, 413–428.

Iimura, H. (2007). The listening process: Effects of types and repetition. *Language Education and Technology 44*, 75–85.

Irving, J. (1978). *The world according to Garp*. New York: Pocket Books.

Jacobs, G., & Small, J. (2003). Combining dictogloss and cooperative learning to promote language learning. *Reading Matrix 3*(1), 1–15.

Jenks, C.J. (2009). Exchanging missing information in tasks: Old and new interpretations. *Modern Language Journal 93*, 185–194.

Jensen, E.D., & Vinther, T. (2003). Exact repetition as input enhancement in second language acquisition. *Language Learning 53*, 373–428.

Johnson, K. (1998). Authenticity. In K. Johnson, & H. Johnson. (Eds.), *Encyclopedic dictionary of applied linguistics* (pp. 24–25). Oxford, U.K.: Blackwell.

Jones, L.C., & Plass, J.L. (2002). Supporting listening comprehension and vocabulary acquisition in French with multimedia annotations. *Modern Language Journal 86*, 546–561.

Jung, E.H. (2003a). The effects of organization markers on ESL learners' text understanding. *TESOL Quarterly 37*, 749–759.

Jung, E.H. (2003b). The role of discourse signaling cues in second language listening comprehension. *Modern Language Journal 87*, 562–577.

Jung, E.H. (2006). Misunderstandings of academic monologues by nonnative speakers of English. *Journal of Pragmatics 38*, 1928–1942.

Kang, O. (2010). Relative salience of suprasegmental features on judgments of L2 comprehensibility and accentedness. *System 38*, 301–315.

Kasper, G., & Kellerman, E. (Eds.). (1997). *Communication strategies: Psycholinguistic and sociolinguistic perspectives*. London: Longman.

Kasper, G. (1997). Beyond reference. In G. Kasper, & E. Kellerman. (Eds.), *Communication strategies: Psycholinguistic and sociolinguistic perspectives* (pp. 345–360). London: Longman.

Keck, C.M., Iberri-Shea, G., Tracy-Ventura, N., & Wa-Mbaleka, S. (2006). Investigating the empirical link between task-based interaction and acquisition: A meta-analysis. In J.M.Norris & L. Ortega. (Eds.), *Synthesizing research on language learning and teaching* (pp. 91–131). Amsterdam: John Benjamins.

Kelch, K. (1985). Modified input as an aid to comprehension. *Studies in Second Language Acquisition 7*, 81–90.

Kelly, P. (1991). Lexical ignorance: The main obstacle to listening comprehension with advanced foreign language learners. *IRAL 29*, 135–149.

Kiany, G.R., & Shiramiry, E. (2002). The effect of frequent dictation on the listening comprehension ability of elementary EFL learners. *TESL Canada Journal 20*(1), 57–63.

Kim, Y. (2008). The contribution of collaborative and individual tasks to the acquisition of L2 vocabulary. *Modern Language Journal 92*, 114–130.

Kozulin, A. (1998). *Psychological tools: A sociocultural approach to education.* Cambridge, MA: Harvard University Press.

Krashen, S. (1982). *Principles and practice in second language acquisition.* Oxford, U.K.: Pergamon.

Krashen, S. (1996). The case for narrow listening. *System 24*, 97–100.

Kuiken, F., & Vedder, I. (2002). The effect of interaction in acquiring the grammar of a second language. *International Journal of Educational Research 37*, 343–358.

Laufer, B., & Shmueli, K. (1997). Memorizing new words: Does teaching have anything to do with it? *RELC Journal 28*, 89–108.

Lesser, M.J. (2004). The effects of topic familiarity, mode and pausing on second language learners' comprehension and focus on form. *Studies in Second Language Acquisition 26*, 587–615.

Levis, J.M. (2005). Changing contexts and shifting paradigms in pronunciation teaching. *TESOL Quarterly 39*, 369–377.

Long, D. R. (1989). Second language listening comprehension: A schema-theoretic perspective. *Modern Language Journal 73*, 32–40.

Long, D.R. (1990). What you don't know can't help you: An exploratory study of background knowledge and second language listening comprehension. *Studies in Second Language Acquisition 12*, 65–80.

Long, M.H. (1996). The role of the linguistic environment in second language acquisition. In W.C. Ritchie & T.K. Bhatia (Eds.). *Handbook of second language acquisition* (pp.413–468). San Diego: Academic Press.

Long, M.H., & Ross, S. (1993). Modifications that preserve language and content. In M.L. Tickoo (Ed.), *Simplification: Theory and application* (pp. 29–52). Singapore: SEAMCO Regional Language Centre.

Loschky, L. (1994). Comprehensible input and second language acquisition: What's the relationship? *Studies in Second Language Acquisition 16*, 303–323.

Lund, R. J. (1990). A taxonomy for teaching second language listening. *Foreign Language Annals 23*(2), 105–115.

Lund, R. (1991). A comparison of second language listening and reading. *Modern Language Journal 75*, 196–204.

Lynch, T. (1995). The development of interactive listening strategies in second language academic settings. In D.J. Mendelsohn, & J. Rubin (Eds.), *A guide for the teaching of second language listening* (pp. 166–185). San Diego: Dominie Press.

Lynch, T. (1997). Life in the slow lane: Observations of a limited L2 listener. *System 25*, 385–393.

Lynch, T. (1998). Theoretical perspectives on listening. *Annual Review of Applied Linguistics 18*, 3–19.

Lynch, T. (2001). Seeing what they meant: Transcribing as a route to noticing. *ELT Journal 55*, 124–132.

Lynch, T., & Maclean, J. (2001). 'A case of exercising': Effects of immediate task repetition on learners' performance. In M. Bygate, P. Skehan, & M. Swain (Eds.), *Researching pedagogical tasks:second language learning, teaching and testing* (pp. 141–165). Harlow, U.K.: Longman.

Macaro, E. (2006). Strategies for language learning and for language use: Revising the theoretical framework. *Modern Language Journal 90*, 320–337.

Mackey, A. (Ed.). (2007). *Conversational interaction in second language acquisition: A collection of empirical studies.* Oxford, U.K.: Oxford University Press.

Mackey, A., & Goo, J. (2007). Interaction research in SLA: A meta-analysis and research synthesis. In A. Mackey (Ed.), *Conversational interaction in second language acquisitions: A collection of empirical studies* (pp. 407–452). Oxford, U.K.: Oxford University Press.

MacWhinney, B. (2001). The competition model: the input, the context, and the brain. In P. Robinson (Ed.), *Cognition and second language instruction* (pp. 69–90). Cambridge, U.K.: Cambridge University Press.

Magnan, S. S. (Ed.). (2007). *Focus Issue of Modern Language Journal 91.*

Major, R.C., Fitzmaurice, S.M., Bunta, F., & Balasubramanian, C. (2002). The effects of nonnative accents on listening comprehension: Implications for ESL assessment. *TESOL Quarterly 36*, 173–190.

Major, R.C., S.M. Fitzmaurice, F. Bunta, & C. Balasubramanian. (2005). Testing the effects of regional, ethnic, and international dialects of English on listening comprehension. *Language Learning 55*, 37–69.

Markham, P., & Latham, M. (1987). The influence of religion-specific background knowledge on the listening comprehension of adult second-language students. *Language Learning 37*, 157–170.

Markham, P. (1999). Captioned videotapes and second-language listening word recognition. *Foreign Language Annals 32*, 321–328.

Markham, P.L., Peter, L.A., & McCarthy, T.J. (2001). The effects of native language vs. target language captions on foreign language students' DVD video comprehension. *Foreign Language Annals 34*, 439–445.

Markham, P., & Peter, L. (2003). The influence of English language and

Spanish language captions on foreign language listening/reading comprehension. *Journal of Educational Technology Systems 31*, 331–341.

Mecartty, F.H. (2000). Lexical and grammatical knowledge in reading and listening comprehension by foreign language learners of Spanish. *Applied Language Learning 11*(2), 323–348.

Mecartty, F. (2001). The effects of modality, information type and language experience on recall by foreign language learners of Spanish. *Hispania 84*, 265–278.

Meinardi, M. (2009). Speed bumps for authentic listening material. *ReCALL 21*, 302–318.

Mendelsohn, D.J., & Rubin, J. (Eds.). (1995). *A guide for the teaching of second language listening.* San Diego: Dominie Press.

Mehrpour, S., & Rahimi, M. (2010). The impact of general and specific vocabulary knowledge on reading and listening comprehension: A case of Iranian EFL learners. *System 38*, 292–300.

Mills, N., Pajares, F., & Herron, C. (2006). A reevaluation of the role of anxiety: Self-efficacy, anxiety, and their relation to reading and listening proficiency. *Foreign Language Annals 39*, 276–295.

Mishan, F. (2004). Authenticating corpora for language learning: a problem and its resolution. *ELT Journal 58*, 219–227.

Mishan, F. & Strunz, B. (2003). An application of XML to the creation of an interactive resource for authentic language learning tasks. *ReCALL 15*, 237–250.

Mondada, L., & Perarek Doehler, S. (2004). Second language acquisition as situated practice: Task accomplishment in the French second language classroom. *Modern Language Journal 88*, 501–518.

Morell, T. (2004). Interactive lecture discourse for university EFL students. *English for Specific Purposes 23*, 325–338.

Morgan, J., & Rinvolucri, M. (1983). *Once upon a time: Using stories in the language classroom.* Cambridge, U.K.: Cambridge University Press.

Morley, J. (1972). *Improving aural comprehension.* Ann Arbor: University of Michigan Press.

Mueller, G.A. (1980). Visual context clues and listening comprehension: An experiment. *Modern Language Journal 64*, 335–340.

Nakahama, Y., Tyler, A., & van Lier, L. (2001). Negotiation of meaning in conversational and information gap activities: A comparative discourse analysis. *TESOL Quarterly 35*, 377–405.

Nation, I.S.P. (2001). *Teaching vocabulary in another language.* Cambridge, U.K.: Cambridge University Press.

Nation, I.S.P. (2006). How large a vocabulary is needed for reading and listening? *The Canadian Modern Language Review 63*, 59–82.

Nunan, D. (2004). *Task-based language teaching.* Cambridge, U.K.: Cambridge University Press.

Nunan, D. (1989). *Designing tasks for the communicative classroom.* Cambridge, U.K.: Cambridge University Press.

Olsen, L.A., & Huckin, T.N. (1990). Point-driven understanding in engineering lecture comprehension. *English for Specific Purposes 9*, 33–47.

O'Malley, J. M., & Chamot, A.U. (1990). *Learning strategies in second language acquisition.* Cambridge, U.K.: Cambridge University Press.

O'Malley J.M., Chamot, A.U., & Küpper, L. (1989). Listening comprehension strategies in second language acquisition. *Applied Linguistics 10*, 418–437.

Park, G. (2004). Comparison of L2 listening and reading comprehension by university students learning English in Korea. *Foreign Language Annals 37*, 448–458.

Pica, T.,Young, R., & Doughty, C. (1987). The impact of interaction on comprehension. *TESOL Quarterly 21*, 737–758.

Pica, T., Kanagy, R., & Falodun, J. (1993). Choosing and using communication tasks for second language instruction and research. In G. Crookes, & S.M. Gass. (Eds.), *Tasks and language learning: Integrating theory and practice* (pp. 9–34). Clevedon, U.K.: Multilingual Matters.

Qin, J. (2008). The effect of processing instruction and dictogloss tasks on acquisition of the English passive voice. *Language Teaching Research 12*, 61–82.

Read, J. (2000). *Assessing vocabulary.* Cambridge, U.K.: Cambridge University Press.

Reinders, H. (2009). Learner uptake and acquisition in three grammar-oriented production activities. *Language Teaching Research 13*, 201–222.

Renandya, W.A., & Farrell, T.S.C. (in press). 'Teacher, the tape is too fast': Extensive listening in ELT. *ELT Journal.*

Richards, J. C. (1983). Listening comprehension: Approach, design, procedure. *TESOL Quarterly 17*, 219–240.

Richards, J.C. (2001). *Curriculum development in language teaching.* Cambridge, U.K.: Cambridge University Press.

Richards, J.C. (2005). Second thoughts on teaching listening. *RELC Journal 36*(1), 85–92.

Ridgway, T. (2000). Listening strategies—I beg your pardon? *ELT Journal 54*, 179–185.

Roberts, C. (1996). A social perspective on understanding: Some issues of theory and method. In K. Bremer, C. Roberts, M. Vasseur, M. Simonot, & P. Broeder (Eds.), *Achieving understanding: Discourse in intercultural encounters* (pp. 9–36). London: Longman.

Roberts, C., & Cooke, M. (2009). Authenticity in the adult ESOL classroom and beyond. *TESOL Quarterly 43*, 620–642.

Robin, R. (2007). Commentary: Learner-based listening and technological authenticity. *Language Learning & Technology 11*, 109–115. Retrieved from http://llt.msu.edu/vol1num1/robin. Accessed August 27, 2010.

Robinson, P. (2001). (Ed.). *Cognition and second language instruction.* Cambridge, U.K.: Cambridge University Press.

Robinson, P. (2001). Task complexity, cognitive resources, and syllabus design: A triadic framework for examining task influences on SLA. In P. Robinson (Ed.), *Cognition and second language instruction* (pp. 287–318). Cambridge, U.K.: Cambridge University Press.

Rost, M. (1990). *Listening in language learning.* London: Longman.

Rost, M. (2002). *Teaching and researching listening.* Harlow, U.K.: Longman.

Rost, M. & Ross, S. (1991). Learner use of strategies in interaction: Typology and teachability. *Language Learning 41*, 235–268.

Rubin, J. (1995). The contribution of video to the development of competence in listening. In D. Mendelsohn and J. Rubin (Eds.), *A guide for the teaching of second language listening* (pp. 151–165). San Diego: Dominie Press.

Ruddell, R.B., Ruddell, M.R., & Singer, H. (Eds.) (1994). *Theoretical models and processes of reading, 4th edition.* Newark, DE: International Reading Association.

Sakai, H. (2009). Effect of repetition of exposure and proficiency level in L2 listening tests. *TESOL Quarterly 43*, 360–372.

Schank, R.C., & Abelson, R.P. (1977). *Scripts, plans, goals and understanding: An enquiry into human knowledge structure.* Hillsdale, NJ: Lawrence Erlbaum.

Schmidt, R. (2001). Attention. In P. Robinson (Ed.), *Cognition and second language instruction* (pp. 3–32). Cambridge, U.K.: Cambridge University Press.

Schmidt-Rinehart, B. C. (1994). The effects of topic familiarity on second language listening comprehension. *Modern Language Journal 78*, 179–189.

Skehan, P. (2003). Task-based instruction. *Language Teaching 36*, 1–14.

Smith, G. P. (2003). Music and mondegreens: Extracting meaning from noise. *ELT Journal 57*, 113–121.

Song, M-Y. (2008). Do divisible subskills exist in second language (L2) comprehension? A structural equation modeling approach. *Language Testing 25*, 435–464.

Staehr, L.S. (2009). Vocabulary knowledge and advanced listening comprehension in English as a foreign language. *Studies in Second Language Acquisition 31*, 577–607.

Stanovich, K. (1980). Toward an interactive-compensatory model of individual differences in the acquisition of literacy. *Reading Research Quarterly 16*, 32–71.

Stewart, M., & Pertusa, I. (2004). Gains to language learners from viewing target language closed-captioned films. *Foreign Language Annals 37*, 438–442.

Sticht, T.G., & James, J.H. (2002/1984). Listening and reading. In P. David Pearson (Ed.), *Handbook of reading research* (pp. 293–318). Mahwah, NJ: Lawrence Erlbaum.

Sueyoshi, A., & Hardison, D.M. (2005). The role of gestures and facial cues in second language listening comprehension. *Language Learning 55*, 661–699.

Swain. M. (2000). The output hypothesis and beyond: Mediating acquisition through collaborative dialogue. In J.P. Lantolf (Ed.), *Sociocultural theory and second language learning* (pp. 97–114). Oxford, U.K.: Oxford University Press.

Swain, M., & Lapkin, S. (1995). Problems in output and the cognitive processes they generate: A step towards second language learning. *Applied Linguistics 16*, 371–391.

Swain, M., & Lapkin, S. (2001). Focus on form through collaborative dialogue: Exploring task effects. In M. Bygate, P. Skehan, & M. Swain (Eds.), *Researching pedagogical tasks: Second language learning, teaching and testing* (pp. 99–118). Harlow, U.K.: Longman.

Taguchi, N. (2005). Comprehending implied meaning in English as a foreign language. *Modern Language Journal 89*, 543–562.

Taguchi, N. (2008). Pragmatic comprehension in Japanese as a foreign language. *Modern Language Journal 92*, 558–576.

Tauroza, S. (1993). Recognizing words in continuous speech: How important are word-final consonants? *ELT Journal 47*, 211–218.

Tauroza, S., & Allison, D. (1990). Speech rates in British English. *Applied Linguistics 11*, 90–105.

Tauroza, S., & Allison, D. (1994). Expectation-driven understanding in information systems lecture comprehension. In J. Flowerdew (Ed.), *Academic listening: Research perspectives* (pp. 35–54). Cambridge, U.K.: Cambridge University Press.

Tauroza, S., & Luk, J. (1997). Accent and second language listening comprehension. *RELC Journal 28*, 54–71.

Taylor, G. (2005). Perceived processing strategies of students watching captioned video. *Foreign Language Annnals 38*, 422–427.

Thompson, S.E. (2003). Text-structuring metadiscourse, intonation and the signaling of organization in academic lectures. *Journal of English for Academic Purposes 2*, 5–20.

Thompson, I., & Rubin, J. (1996). Can strategy instruction improve listening comprehension? *Foreign Language Annals 29*, 331–342.

Thornbury, S. (1997). Reformulation and reconstruction: Tasks that promote 'noticing.' *ELT Journal 51*, 326–335.

Tomlinson, B. (Ed.). (2003). *Developing materials for language teaching.* London: Continuum.

Tsui, A.B.M., & Fullilove, J. (1998). Bottom-up or top-down processing as a discrimination of L2 listening performance. *Applied Linguistics 19*, 432–451.

Tudor, I., & Tuffs, R. (1991). Formal and content schemata activation in L2 viewing comprehension. *RELC Journal 22*, 79–97.

Tyler, M.D. (2001). Resource consumption as a function of topic knowledge in nonnative and native comprehension. *Language Learning 51*, 257–280.

Ur, P. (1984). *Teaching listening comprehension.* Cambridge, U.K.: Cambridge University Press.

Vandergrift, L. (1997a). The comprehension strategies of second language (French) listeners: A descriptive study. *Foreign Language Annals 30*, 387–409.

Vandergrift, L. (1997b). The Cinderella of communication strategies: Reception strategies in interactive listening. *Modern Language Journal 81*, 494–505.

Vandergrift, L. (2003a). Orchestrating strategy use: Toward a model of the skilled second language listener. *Language Learning 53*, 463–496.

Vandergrift, L. (2003b). From prediction through reflection: Guiding students through the process of L2 listening. *The Canadian Modern Language Review 59*, 425–440.

Vandergrift, L. (2006). Second language listening: Listening ability or language proficiency? *The Modern Language Journal 90*, 6–18.

Vandergrift, L., & Tafaghodtari, M.H. (2010). Teaching L2 learners how to listen does make a difference: An empirical study. *Language Learning 60*, 470–497.

Vanderplank, R. (2010). Déjà vu? A decade of research on language labs, TV and video in language teaching. *Language Teaching 43*, 1–37.

VanPatten, B. (1996). *Input processing and grammar instruction: Theory and research*. Norwood, NJ: Ablex Publishing.

VanPatten, B., Inclezan, D., Salazar, H., & Farley, A.P. (2009). Processing instruction and dictogloss: A study on object pronouns and word order in Spanish. *Foreign Language Annals 42*, 557–575.

Vogely, A. (1995). Perceived strategy use during performance on three authentic listening comprehension tasks. *Modern Language Journal 79*, 41–56.

Voss, B. (1979). Hesitation phenomena as sources of perceptual errors for non-native speakers. *Language and Speech 22*(2), 129–144.

Vygotsky, L.S. (1978). *Mind in society: The development of higher psychological processes*. Cambridge, MA: Harvard University Press.

Wajnryb, R. (1990). *Grammar dictation*. Oxford, U.K.: Oxford University Press.

Waring, R. (2010). Starting extensive listening. Retrieved from http://www.robwaring.org//el/starting_extensive_listening.htm. Accessed May 24, 2010.

Watanabe, Y. (2008). Peer-peer interaction between L2 learners of different proficiency levels: Their interactions and reflections. *Canadian Modern Language Review 64*, 605–635.

Weber, A., & Cutler, A. (2006). First-language phonotactics in second-language listening. *Journal of the Acoustical Society of America 119*(1), 597–607.

Weissenreider, M. (1987). Listening to the news in Spanish. *Modern Language Journal 71*, 18–27.

Weyers, J.R. (1999). The effect of authentic video on communicative competence. *Modern Language Journal 83*, 339–349.

Widdowson, H.G. (1979). *Explorations in applied linguistics*. Oxford, U.K.: Oxford University Press.

Widdowson, H.G. (1998). Context, community, and authentic language. *TESOL Quarterly 32*, 705–716.

Wilberschied, L., & Berman, P.M. (2004). Effect of using photos from authentic video as advance organizers on listening comprehension of an FLES Chinese class. *Foreign Language Annals, 37*, 534–540.

Wilson, M. (2003). Discovery listening: Improving perceptual processing. *ELT Journal 57*, 335–343.

Wolff, D. (1987). Some assumptions about second language text comprehension. *Studies in Second Language Acquisition 9*, 307–326.

Wong, J. (2002). Applying conversation analysis in applied linguistics: Evaluating dialogue in English as a second language. *IRAL 40*, 37–60.

Woodall, B. (2010). Simultaneous listening and reading in ESL: Helping second language learners read (and enjoy reading) more efficiently.

TESOL Journal 1, 186–205. Retrieved from http://tesol.publisher. ingentaconnect.com/content/tesol/tjnew/2010/00000001/00000002 /art00004. Accessed August 26, 2010.

Works, N.M. (1985). Materials used for the teaching of listening comprehension: A survey. *TESOL Newsletter 12*(6), 27, 29.

Wright, S. (1954). The death of Lady Mondegreen. *Harper's Magazine 209*(1254), 48–51.

Wu, Y. (1998). What do tests of listening comprehension test? A retrospection study of EFL test-takers performing a multiple-choice task. *Language Testing 15*, 21–44.

Yanagawa, K. & Green, A. (2008). To show or not to show: The effects of item stems and answer options on performance on a multiple-choice listening comprehension test. *System 36*, 107–122.

Zhao, Y. (1997). The effects of listeners' control of speech rate on second language comprehension. *Applied Linguistics 18*, 49–68.

Zielinski, B.W. (2008). The listener: No longer the silent partner in reduced intelligibility. *System 36*, 69–84.

Subject Index

accent, 56, 57, 64–65, 68-70, 76
annotations, 90
anxiety, 9, 74, 76, 138, 162
assessment, 9–10, 51, 56, 69–70, 165
attention, 54, 55, 57, 93, 154, 162
authenticity, 132–137, 140–145
authentic materials: defined, 135–136; textbooks compared to, 136–137; technology and, 139–140, 145, 148; used in classrooms, 74, 85, 133, 135; used in research studies, 22, 27, 66, 72, 90; why effective, 66, 134, 138–139

back channel cues, 4, 109, 124
background knowledge. *See* schemata
bottom-up processing, vii, 19, 20, 29, 30–34, 36, 37–47

captions, 8, 12, 85, 87–91
cognates, 3, 4, 7
cognitive models, 18–20, 112–115
collocations, 38
comprehension process: bottom-up processing and, 37–40; defined, 6, 9–10, 18–20; improving, 68; in listening vs. reading, 7–11, 21;

interaction and, 112–115; learners' perceived problems with, 54–57; pre-listening activities and, 24–27, 29–34; speech rate and, 63–66; text structure and, 27–28; vocabulary and, 57–63
comprehension questions, 2, 8, 36, 50, 56
content schemata, 19, 20, 27, 28
content words, 41–42, 46
context, 5, 10, 24, 37, 38, 55, 154, 157, 159
co-text, 10, 37, 75
corpora, 58–60, 139, 148

decoding, 10, 11, 37, 38, 47
details: as aspect of linguistic comprehension, 72; compared to main ideas, 39, 62, 153; in classroom activities, 77, 78, 80, 82, 83; in reading vs. listening, 7–11, 13, 61; lecture listening and, 97, 98; repetition and, 27
dialogues, 13, 15–16, 75, 84
dictations: as classroom activities, 49, 50, 83, 101–103, 157; in research studies, 46, 85, 91–96
dictogloss, 92, 93, 94, 95, 103–104
discourse markers, 96–99, 161

Author Index